Believing the HYPE

7 Keys to motivating students of color

Darrell "Coach D" Andrews

Speaker, Consultant and Author
Darrell Andrews Enterprises
FamQuest, Inc.

Foreword by Dr. Jawanza Kunjufu

HYPE™, Connecting Dreams To Education™ and Passion Map™ are trademarks of Darrell Andrews Enterprises

Darrell Andrews Enterprises
1148 Pulaski Hwy
Ste. 197
Bear, DE 19701

ISBN: 0-9660103-5-3

LCCN: 2004099723

Tele: 302-834-1040
Email: info@coachdspeaks.com
Web: www.coachdspeaks.com

Printed in the United States of America

Contents

Acknowledgements

Without my wife Pamela, I would not be where I am today. She is the greatest gift God has given me. She is my love, my queen as well as my soul mate. She believes in the vision I have for transformation and change, and is the backbone behind the success of our company. We have built this organization together and stand strong as a husband and wife united. She is a remarkable teacher, mother, businesswoman and mentor to young ladies. As I am preparing this book, she is daily researching ways for our company to have greater impact. She is the most amazing, highly motivated woman I know. In her own right she could have succeeded in the engineering field (she has a degree in Electrical Engineering from North Carolina A&T State University), but she chose to pursue our dream, our passion. I love her with all of my heart. My wife and I were told by many physicians that we could not have children. However, after years of prayer, we now are blessed to have three of the greatest children on the planet: Darrell Jr, Sophia, and Alexander. I thank them for bringing a smile to Daddy's face every time I walk through the door. I would also like to acknowledge Dr. Myles Munroe who first introduced me to passion and purpose. His life and words have impacted me more than any other speaker and author. Dr. George Fraser, who I met while speaking at an Economic Summit, encouraged me to impact as many lives as possible with the message of passion, and he backed up his statement by inviting me to speak at his nationally recognized *PowerNetworking Conference.* My thanks to Earl Stafford, President of UniTech, Inc in Centerville, VA who took the time to share words of wisdom despite having an extremely busy schedule running a successful technology firm. I am grateful to Tavis Smiley for his support of our work on the radio and television media as well as his work impacting the next generation of leaders through the Tavis Smiley Foundation. My interview on his show touched thousands of lives nationally. My staff constantly supports our efforts, and I am grateful. To Linda Haskins, my editor, my deepest gratitude. I also express gratitude to Mark Chamberlin, from the Delaware Department of Education with whom it has been a pleasure to work in the area of motivating special education students and students with disabilities. Thanks also to the numerous schools, organizations and associations who invite me to speak at their conferences and events annually. I appreciate the efforts of Comcast's CN8 *Your Morning* team, and in particular, Cathy Ballou for having me appear as a regular guest on their morning program. Further, I acknowledge with appreciation Regina Greenwald, Jackie Norman, Hazel Showell, The Parent Information Center, Tom Smith and Michael Benefield, Vera Hextall-Gear Up Director, The National Alliance of Black School Educators-NABSE, Superintendent Clarence Hoover, Nancy White, Joyce Kaufmann, Debra and Victor Williams, Chancellor Martha Russell of Raising Horizons Quest Charter School, Maurice Stewart from the U.S. Department of Education's Intergovernmental Affairs Office, Marty Young from Foundations, Inc., Joyce Henderson, Assistant Director MBNA Career Services at the University of Delaware, my colleagues at NSA and many others. Without the synergy of advocates and supporters, dreams would not have come true. Thanks to all for their on-going support of the mission of FamQuest and Darrell Andrews Enterprises.

Foreword

By Dr. Jawanza Kunjufu

Author of *Black Students Middle Class Teachers*

Coach Darrell Andrews has written a very empowering book, *"Believing the HYPE: Seven Keys to Motivating Students of Color".* He has lived up to his title "coach". I argue that our children need coaches, e.g. master teachers. *Believing the HYPE* is a very comprehensive book ideal for teachers, parents, and students. The seven keys include Connecting Dreams to Education, Passionizing your Delivery, Developing Student Councils, Purging the Past, Understanding the Changing Times, Bridging the Parent Gap, and Developing Goals and Measurements.

Darrell Andrews is the epitome of passion-izing your delivery. Today's youth are bombarded by media who have passion. Educators must do the same in their lesson plans. Andrews is very concerned about the racial achievement gap and holds everyone accountable. There is an excellent chapter for students on developing student councils for empowerment. Coach also feels we need to make parents feel important. This is a must read for anyone who cares about children.

Preface

With tears in her eyes she boldly proclaimed, "Coach D, I finally realize that I am a role model." She cried for about twenty minutes and individuals in the workshop simply embraced her as they were moved with compassion. The young lady proclaimed that her life had been in shambles due to family tragedies, and she really did not have any role models to show her how to do things the right way. She stated that because of the challenges she faced in her upbringing, she chose a path that was familiar to her. As a result of going through a comprehensive leadership institute that my company was contracted to develop, she realized that she was now a role model to her younger siblings and she did not want to reproduce the images that caused her to end up in a precarious position. A young man sat there in a daze as we were developing the youth council for his high school. Many thought that he was not paying attention; however, I knew better. I asked him "What is on your mind?" He responded by saying "Coach D, I have been a leader for years in the wrong arena, nobody ever told me I could lead in a positive way. I can't believe that I am now seeing things this way." "I can be whatever I want to be, but it is up to me." Another young lady wrote a letter from college saying, "Thank you for exposing me to a world which I once could have never imagined." Another letter from a young man stated, "I want to be just like you when I grow up." A group of special education students we worked with wrote a poster card for the birth of my daughter which read, "With you as her Daddy, we know she will succeed." Most of the aforementioned youth in some way were labeled as "at-risk," "special education," "or hard-to-serve." Eighty percent of them are students of color.

There is hope. Hope comes from the heart. Too many people throughout the world have developed perceptions about students of color that are totally incorrect. Many of these perceptions come from media propaganda and labeling based upon a few negative experiences. There are many Black and Latino students who have the seed of greatness inside of them just waiting to sprout. They simply need someone to believe in their future and communicate this to them as often as possible. Schools have the greatest opportunity to provide impact, since for twelve years of the students' life, the classroom has more of their time than anything else. Imagine if we could paint a vision of our expected outcomes for the students and work towards the goals until we see them happening. Today we have No Child Left Behind Legislation and a myriad of Closing the Achievement Gap events throughout the United States. The question we have to ask ourselves is: will they work? Is their enough heart-felt commitment from individuals who work with our children to stay the course until we see tangible success? (Not just statistics and research analysis that are not evident in our day to day lives, however a visual representation of success such as entire school climates changing, relationships in the classroom improving, students dreaming, and connecting their dreams to education.) This is not an overnight proposition, but it is one that is achievable. I sincerely believe whatever a group of people put their minds to, they can accomplish. It is my hope in writing this book that we will create an educational community who is passionate about seeing students of color succeed academically, socially and professionally, changing the many negative perceptions that individuals may have about our students and bridging the racial gap so that we can see all of our students as equal. As we are swiftly becoming a global economy and a global society, we need to look at all of the resources available to keep us competitive. We need to get over the color barrier and prepare the next generation to keep us strong and competitive in a global society. If we do not, where will we be years from now?

I know that there are many educators who are committed. Having been in the trenches in our schools, I have watched teachers pour their hearts out trying to get their students, all of their students, to see the importance of an education. Realize from the onset, I do understand. I have been in meetings where principals have shed tears while they were looking for answers; I have held teachers in my arms as they were crying because they had been wounded by the abrasive words used by some of their students, (not just students of color) and burdened with administrative pressure to meet various standards. Educating today's youth across the board can be a challenge. Generation Y students can be daunting, to say the least. The key is to work from your heart and stay committed to the vision that you have for your students. You chose this profession because of your love for educating the next generation of leaders. All students need you to stay committed to this mission. Students of color especially need people who can pull out the potential within. It is my fondest hope that *Believing the HYPE* will provide you with specific information relating to this quest.

Introduction

The eyes are the window to the soul. No matter what a person shows on the outside, it is what is on the inside that counts. After years of standing on countless school, association and organization stages conducting motivational speeches and rallies, conducting in-class workshops, staff development in-services, as well as one-on-one coaching programs, I am convinced more than ever that there is the seed of academic and personal excellence in our students of color. I can see it in their eyes and in the eyes of many who are in the trenches with them day after day. As I travel the country speaking at various conferences on the topic of motivating youth, I share with my audiences that my focus is never on negative perceptions, but what our children can become. State after state, city after city, and now, nation after nation I hear school districts, superintendents, curriculum directors, board members, principals and teachers share how the achievement gap is widening between students of color and their Caucasian and Asian counterparts, and this is becoming a chronic and critical situation. My general response is "seek to understand." Seek to understand why this is a nationwide problem: what are the reasons this is happening to a particular segment of the population with such magnitude? Seek to understand the cultural differences. Seek to understand the interpersonal challenges your students may be facing. Seek to understand why many organizations do not commit to long-term programs that will bridge the gap between students of color and academic, personal and social excellence. Seek to understand why this is only now becoming a priority when this has been a problem for quite a while now. Seek to understand how we can bridge the gap between educators and parents of color.

Please do not assume by my writings that I believe all students of color fall into the lower achievement category. There are many young people who are excellent students and community leaders. We have personally worked with many outstanding young people. I am saying we do have a nationwide problem that needs to be addressed and not overlooked. This book will provide solutions primarily to schools and school districts which have students who are falling under the curve of academic and social progress and discuss the environments in which they live on a day-to-day basis. If yours is a non-profit agency, after school program or other form of youth organization, some of the information shared can be of assistance to you as well.

Our HYPE (Helping Youth Pursue Excellence) Program has received national recognition for its ability to help students overcome interpersonal barriers to academic, social and personal success. Our primary thrust from day one was focusing on the interpersonal. We never bought into the stereotypical labels that were placed on students who are challenged. Instead, we focused on their potential and their potential only. We realized that motivation plays an important role in the change process; motivation is the spark that ignites the fire of creativity. By providing them with a picture of hope for their future, and the necessary motivation to accomplish their dreams, students of color can overcome any obstacle to academic and personal success.

I know this first hand because I was labeled as a child. People predicted that I would not accomplish anything with my life. Even a close family member told me that white America would never support my ideas, so I was advised to get a job in the factory. I have personally experienced racial divide that caused me to look at things in a negative way and was told that this country does not support dreamers who are of African descent. When I was in college I stopped by my bank one day in Media, PA to withdraw money for lunch (back then they did not have ATM's.)

While standing in line, I noticed seven or eight police cars surrounding the bank. Fearing the bank was being robbed, I stood still in line hoping that the robber would not pull out a gun and start shooting. To my surprise, the police barged into the bank, grabbed me out of the line, handcuffed me and slammed me against the wall. I was in total shock, wondering "Why are they doing this to me? What did I do? I have never committed a crime in my life, I will go to jail for no reason, I will not finish college, my life is ruined forever!" I asked the police officer that had me in handcuffs what he thought I had done. He pointed his finger in my face and shouted "Shut your mouth or I will slam you in jail!" Stunned and confused, I wondered: Why were they doing this to me? When the Chief of Police walked in a few moments later, I then knew this was something extremely serious. He went into a back room with the bank manager. (Keep in mind that I was the only African-American in the bank.) A few moments later they emerged from the room and the Chief told the officer to "un-cuff him." I asked the police officer "what just happened?" He turned belligerently and repeated with his finger pointing in my face, "I told you to shut your mouth or I am going to slam your butt in jail!" I was absolutely baffled! I eventually went over to the bank manager and asked, "What just happened?" She said "Mr. Andrews we are sorry but it was a case of mistaken identity." Based upon this experience, my thoughts of racism exploded. A similar experience took place in the same town back in the early 80's when I was almost arrested for mistaken identity when entering an apartment complex in which I lived. Had you met me then, you would have labeled me as a young black male with an anger management problem and no future. To the contrary, I was a good young man raised by a mother who instilled good values in my brother and me from an early age. You may have labeled me rebellious even in the classroom, but inside of me was a powerful seed of potential. I was simply influenced by a very negative experience. Thousands of children of color sitting in classrooms all over the country have experienced this and similar situations. Their situations may not have been identical to mine; however they may have experienced other life-polluting experiences stemming perhaps from generational beliefs that people of color cannot succeed as a whole (in the United States in particular),or that school is not important because it has not benefited anyone in their community or family. *If you do not know your students from the heart, you will make assumptions that will limit their possibilities forever.* I once spoke to a man who said that he was told by his 11th grade teacher "you will never amount to anything in life." At the age of 48 those prophetic words were evident in his life. He told me that shaking her words has been a life long quest. As educators, your words, which are typically derived from your perceptions of people, have tremendous, reverberating power. Once you change any negative perceptions, you can change your students' reality.

My mother, a master motivator, taught me that I could grow up to become whatever I wanted to be; that I could live my dreams and pursue my goals. Reminding me that the town in which we were living at the time was not the limit of my possibilities, she told me to go and carve out a future for myself; there is a big world out there filled with opportunities to be shaped by those who are willing to do the carving. I did not have to live in a quagmire; I could, as they say in the Army, be all that I could be. This constant motivation coupled with the support of people like my 6th grade teacher Ms. Palma, my 8th grade teacher Mr. Miller, and my college football Coach Andrew Henson, caused me to be the first person in my family to graduate with a bachelor's degree, the first one to work for a major corporation, the first to excel as a business owner, regularly sought after for radio and television interviews, and as a keynote speaker and trainer. All of this happened because of the power of motivation. The same person, who in his younger years was challenged by negative labeling and bad life experiences, was loved into the right direction. With all of my heart I believe that you have the same ability to positively impact your students' lives. You can fill them everyday with a belief that they are important and their lives count. All of the aforementioned individuals used creative, outside-of-the-box techniques to motivate me. This is why I remember them. I cannot remember the names of most of the other educators, coaches, and staff members because they simply did their job and went home at the end of the day. The other individuals went above and beyond their jobs: they were passionate about making a difference, and, as a result, they did!

Young people can develop based upon the seed of possibility inside them. As an educator, administrator, superintendent, parent or other stakeholder in our children's future, we have the responsibility to believe that it can be done. I am writing this book to provide several keys to help you close the achievement gap and really leave no child behind, and to create young leaders of color who will be viable, powerful contributors to society. You have to believe the HYPE. The HYPE (Helping Youth Pursue Excellence) that:

> ➢ Students of color can excel academically and be leaders.
> ➢ Students of color are and can continue to be valuable assets to our society.
> ➢ Not all students of color are gang bangers, drug dealers and listen to hip-hop music.
> ➢ Many students of color have dreams and ambitions. The key to success is going to be connecting dreams to education.
> ➢ Even though African-Americans and Latinos are called minorities (which the dictionary describes as marginal;

thus I do not use this term) 90% of us were born in this country. We are co-laborers in the building of this nation and the world as a whole. All of our nation's children deserve to be valued equally and have access to quality education.

Unless we begin to change our paradigm about our students of color and make change a part of our organizational infrastructure, we will never change our situation. Perception is reality and we have to perceive that the future is bright for all students, including students of color. *We do not have to revisit this issue ten years from now. We can change it for the better.*

Chapter 1

The HYPE Philosophy

Our company's HYPE Philosophy simply stated is that "All youth have the seed of potential in them despite the negative challenges of their past or present." Our vision statement reads *Transforming the Next Generation Through Passion and Purpose.* We do not look at any young person as hopeless. We believe that even the most difficult youth became that way due to life's circumstances. They did not begin life going down the path that put them in their current situation—life took them there. I jokingly say at many of my keynote presentations that I don't know of one baby that started off life whining:

- ✦ I want to be a problem to my parents.
- ✦ I want to fail miserably at school and life.
- ✦ I want to be mean and cantankerous.
- ✦ I want to live a life in which none of my dreams come true.
- ✦ I want to hate my teachers, parents and all authority figures.

By focusing on the positives and building mutually respectful relationships we believe that parents, educators and youth workers can help youth overcome the challenges of adolescence and grow up to be productive citizens of our society.

There are three target areas that we feel will help young people focus on creating a brighter future. They are:

Relationships—Establish positive friendships in and out
of school. These friendships should be centered
on positive values and future-enhancing.

Identity—Be proud of your heritage, culture and talents.
Each person brings unique gifts to the planet.

Dreams—Create a bright, optimistic future for yourself
based upon goal setting and internal dream belief
system enhancement.

I. Relationships—Recognize that relationships are an important factor in the proper development of youth. In our program we establish codes of ethics that must be adhered to by each student.

Many of the problems youth face are connected to the relationships they develop in and out of school. In the process of helping students develop a positive future, it is essential to help students understand the importance of establishing positive relationships and ending toxic ones.

II. Identity—Many students face an identity crisis. Clearly this is one of the reasons so many young people join gangs. Another challenge that many students face is the racial, gender and age divide between teachers and students. Many educators, from my experiences, have a difficult time understanding the challenges faced by many of their students as a result of one or a combination of these factors.

I define identity as the unique and distinct characteristics of a person. A person who experiences an identity crisis is uncomfortable in his or her unique makeup. Many times he or she lacks a sense of significance or self worth. Students who are proud of their identity and heritage will excel no matter what challenges they encounter.

III. Dreams—Napoleon Hill, Author of *Think and Grow Rich,* states the following about dreams: "Cherish your vision and your dreams, they are the children of your soul; they are the blueprint of your ultimate achievement." We believe that the dreams factor of our philosophy is the most significant. When young people are focused on the endless possibilities that life offers, their identity and their relationships will come into alignment and lead to academic and personal excellence.

Why This Philosophy?

We believe that the interpersonal change process happens over time. The more we focus on building positive human infrastructures within our educational systems and our communities, the more likely we are to increase our chances of student success. Dr. William James, a late 19th and early 20th century Harvard Professor considered by many as one of the greatest philosophers and psychologists of his era, perceived change this way: "The greatest discovery of my generation is a person can alter his life by altering his attitudes of mind." As educators, by possessing the right attitude, you can begin to examine the infinite number of ways to motivate and inspire your students to success in the classroom.

Another reason why we have chosen this philosophy is that negative energy is too often pervasive. A recently published article was entitled "America, Land of the Free and Home of the Rude." Due a decline in values, lack of integrity and capitalistic attitude of many, our great nation is becoming a negative one. Job statistics have proven that the majority of people dislike their jobs, that drug and alcohol abuse continues to escalate, and that the divorce rate is climbing at an alarming rate. With a prodigious amount of negative avenues available, we must work diligently to create and maintain positive highways to success. In order to do this however, one must change their internal environment. You and I must wake up everyday realizing that the work we do requires us to be positive and upbeat. We cannot allow the pressures of life to lead us off course. Our children need to have positive models of stability in the midst of changes and challenges. Such models provide leadership. As parents, educators, administrators, and mentors, we must be leaders by example. This is why we believe in our HYPE philosophy as well as in you. We realize that you—every educator, parent and youth worker—can intentionally improve your internal world and perceptions, thus improving the outcomes of events and people all around you. Your students and co-workers need for you to operate from this frame of reference.

Neither the nation nor the world can do anything effectively without teachers or parents, for without parents there would be no children, and without teachers we would live in a world of illiteracy and minimal intellectual capabilities, doomed to certain, ignominious extinction. Your work is invaluable! Every student in your sphere of influence has the ability to live his or her dreams. This is an attitude you definitely must adopt in order to positively influence all of your students, particularly students of color who are often ignored or underserved.

You Must Have A Philosophy

A philosophy is simply and attitude, viewpoint or way of life. The beauty of having a philosophy is that it acts as a point of measurement for the work you are doing. Every new idea or initiative, as it relates to closing the achievement gap and motivating students of color, needs to have an underlying philosophy connected to the vision statement.

If you are simply doing the job because someone told you to or to simply get paid at the end of the week, your plan will never work. Consider the adage: "For lack of a vision, the people perish." When thinking about what your goals are for your school district, government, organization or association, you need first to think about the reasons for which you are pursuing those quantifiable goals, and you must form a team committed to achieving them. Just as I believe in the potential of the students, I believe in the potential of the school staff. Positive, enduring change is possible; however, it must be worked on regularly and vigorously. Your philosophy can be the starting point of building a successful system.

System Development

As aforementioned, a school-wide philosophy relating to inspiring students of color is critical when considering closing the gap. It is even more critical when considering developing a system around the philosophy. One of the major barriers to goal attainment is the challenge of consistency. Because many organizations lack a solid philosophy or vision, they abandon ideas once they are faced with the challenges in seeing success. Granted, some ideas do need to be aborted. Most great projects take time however. As the old saying goes "Rome was not built in a day", so the topics discussed in this book will not change things overnight. It will take some "sweat equity" to create a system that will cause and inspire your underserved students of color to excel.

Commitment to a system is a necessity because improvement is an on-going process. When looking at ways to motivate students of color, first look at why you are doing it; this is your philosophy. Next, build a cross-functional team that is designed to support this initiative: a team consisting of students, teachers, administrators, counselors, and the like. Identify several goals and a plan of action to achieve them. Make sure that the leadership of the schools is engaged in the process because if the school leaders do not believe in the vision, it will be difficult to get others to believe. A program without leadership buy-in will fail in a short period of time. In order to start the transformation process effectively, your institution must have plans for success built upon a solid philosophy and vision. This is one of the challenges I see that many schools, school districts and organizations face. It is one that is critical relating to outcomes based success in motivating students of color towards academic and personal success.

Chapter Summary

This chapter was designed to provide a foundation for the upcoming chapters. You need to determine a *why* before you can develop a *how*. *In many of the schools to which I am invited, I find that neither a philosophy, nor a vision, nor mission has been established.* I always ask several people to define their mission in one sentence to explain the underlying philosophy behind what they do. Ninety nine percent of the people do not have an answer and those who do are unclear about it. Unity of purpose is important, and in order to see short and long term success, you must have a vision and a philosophy behind the vision. Having these tools, you will be well on your way in the direction of success!

— Chapter One Highlights —

+ Your school or organization must develop a core philosophy.

+ In my company's philosophy we have chosen to believe that all children have the seed of potential in them. We build from this premise.

+ Once the philosophy is in place, it will still take "sweat equity" to see success.

+ You must get leadership buy-in. This is paramount to success.

+ Establish a systems-based approach. You must have a system in place if you expect to succeed.

KEY 1

Connecting Dreams To Education™

Imagine taking a vacation in a foreign country where you do not speak that country's native tongue. You could not purchase gifts because you do not understand the vendor's explanation of the product or its cost. Eating would certainly be a challenge because you would not know what to order, or what the cost would be. Traveling throughout the country might present a challenge because if you got lost, you wouldn't have the resources to ask for directions. After a while it would simply get frustrating, and you would ultimately give up. You were unable to connect with the people because you did not understand their language. A similar phenomenon is occurring in schools nationwide when neither the students nor the educators understand each other. There is a terrible disconnect when each entity is living in a different world, trying to impose their beliefs on one another rather than trying to understand each other. I think of the occasions during which I speak to executives in the educational, organizational or the association community discussing everything from leadership to vision and planning. My language is appropriate for my specific audience. It would not make sense for me to share this same message with a group of middle school students in an assembly because I would lose them in a heartbeat. Since students will not make it a priority to connect with their mentors and teachers, we must be proactive and learn how to better connect with them.

One of the most critical messages that I share with audiences worldwide is that we need to also start **Connecting Dreams To**

Education™. For many young people today, getting good grades merely because they are told they need to do so is not going to cut it. While this may have worked in the 1950's, 1960's, and 1970's, it is simply a fable to them in the new millennium. They are seeing young people of their own generation without even a baccalaureate degree, appearing on television, living in multi-million dollar mansions, and driving luxury vehicles. From their vantage point, education is not necessary to guarantee a successful future. From their perspective, many also see the history of their parents and education, parents who fought hard to get into the schools, only to be deprived of opportunities once they graduated because they were people of color. Segregation and discrimination during that bygone era were not kind to them. Please keep in mind we are talking about a time less than one generation removed from the initial civil rights struggle. We still have a long way to go before we can expect immediate change in mindsets on both sides of the fence. When the change occurs, there will no longer be a fence—no barriers to making the connection.

Another challenge in this struggle is the doubt by minorities that dreams can indeed become reality. If you are part of a culture in which you have models of success reaching back as far as the founding of this nation, this doubt may not make sense to you. But consider that if every generation of your family had to start the process all over again and the only history you have has been one of slavery, submission, and struggle, where would your life be today? If this were a reflection of your history, *could* you have the dreams you have today? Many students of color need to be inspired towards their dreams, for they may have no historical representation of them. Educational institutions can help to connect the dream-line. Listed are some ways of connecting the dreams of your students to education.

1. Talk To Your Students About Their Dreams

I remember years ago in middle school a coach on the football team walked up to me and made the statement, "You are going to be a Renaissance man!" I was in the ninth grade at that time, clueless to the term, so I thought that he was talking about the famous statue of the thinking man. Was he saying that I was going to become a statue? Years went by before I decided to look up the definition of *renaissance.* The power of this man's words were so hauntingly compelling, I was committed to finally getting an understanding of what he meant. The term has several meanings. They are as follows:

- ✦ Revival
- ✦ New Start
- ✦ New Beginning
- ✦ Reawakening
- ✦ Rebirth

His words were precise, on point. My days I now spend providing students, school districts, organizations, associations and individuals with a new beginning, a reawakening, and a revival! Through the power of motivation, I am able to help people get on the right course in life. Words have tremendous power, and by taking the time to connect with the dreams of your students, you will be initiating a process that will have a life long impact. Just as some people's words have been used to destroy dreams, your words can be used to help your students believe they can achieve them. Following are a few suggested exercises.

Exercise # 1—Classroom Rap Sessions

At least once per month allow your students to share their dreams. They can begin the process of creating vision posters by arranging clippings, pictures and statements relating to their dreams on poster board. Using this information, each student can discuss the importance of his or her dream. It is important, however, to create an environment in the classroom that supports this exercise prior to conducting it. Based upon the class size, you may want to consider scheduling the exercise over a few class periods because it is important to give the students ample time to share their thoughts. Some questions to consider for the session are:

1. What is your dream, and how long have you had it?
2. Do you know of anyone who is living this dream?
3. What do you think is going to be the most exciting aspect of living this dream?
4. Class, what can we do to encourage each other towards our dreams? (A great way to get more classroom ideas)
5. What will be the benefits to you, your family and friends once you start to live this dream?
6. In what way can I help you as your teacher (counselor, after school program coordinator etc.) to live your dream?

This is an effective exercise to bring energy and vitality to connecting to the students' life ambitions. It is also a great way to show your students that you care about what is important to them. I have personally conducted this exercise many times, and the student response is still amazing. It is important during this exercise to let the students have fun and be creative. If you show negative personal perceptions, you will damage the spirit behind this exercise designed to help you to better connect to the world of your students by identifying what matters to them. In doing this, you open lines of communication rarely acknowledged by adults to your students.

Exercise # 2—Visual Dream Connections

After identifying some of the dreams the students shared during the first exercise, help students to research newspapers, magazines, old books and the Internet to identify several people (people of color for your students of color) who have accomplished the dreams of the students. Again, cut out pictures, quotes and statements made by these individuals, take a snapshot of your students, create a vision board and post it in the classroom. Add each student's photograph to those of the individuals identified in the dream search, and label each poster:

"<u>Student's Name</u> and His or Her Dream Colleagues."

Regularly make reinforcing comments to them regarding their colleagues and the students' quest to accomplish the dream. This is another fun way to relate to them with the ultimate quest of connecting their dreams to education by encouraging them to stay on their academic course of success.

The aforementioned exercises are proven ways to connect to the dreams of your students. Please keep in mind that the goal here is simply connection. Some of the dreams the students have may seem strange, far-fetched, and difficult to comprehend based upon your knowledge of the students, but remember, many great achievers overcame tremendous odds to succeed. Students will appreciate your willingness to take this fun journey with them. Most importantly, it will open them up to explore other ideas mentioned throughout this book.

2. Identify Resources To Provide Visual Representation Of The Dream

Once you have identified some of their dreams, have the students compile resources to support the dreams. Motivational speakers, community leaders or business leaders are great resources to call upon to provide visual representation of the dreams. The more frequently the students are exposed to real world representations of their dreams, the better their chances for success. This is a paradigm which I am passionate about having schools and organizations adopt nationwide because too many students of color do not see people of their race visually represented in textbooks, stories, in assemblies, or in other forms. When I was sharing this information at a teacher's summer training institute, a Latino teacher in the audience shared with passion and fervor, "I agree Coach D, I agree. I remember in high school the first time I saw a Latino come into the school to provide a motivational program. Of all of the events that I had experienced over my years in school, this event had the most significant impact. By seeing a successful Latino come into my school, I began to realize that I could be a success too!" I believe that teacher's excitement points to the fact that this is an important component in motivating students of color. You can also accomplish this through videos, magazines or other forms of visual stimulation. There are countless culturally specific resources available to assist in your quest.

3. Develop A Passion Map™ To Identify Skill Sets

By far, one of my proudest product development accomplishments as a speaker, trainer, author or consultant is that of developing the Passion Map™. Understanding the power of taking a person's passion and mapping it out can change a life permanently. (I encourage you to consider my book *How To Find Your Passion—A Youth Perspective* for your students to get a fuller explanation of the concept.) In the education process, developing a map for your students is the best way to not only motivate them towards their dreams, but also find the necessary educational skill sets needed to accomplish this dream. For instance, a student who has a passion for sports would have a map that resembles the following:

Passion—Athletics

Career Possibilities

+ Gym Teacher
+ Professional Athlete
+ Sports Agent
+ Sports Therapist
+ Coach

Once you identify the possibilities, have the students narrow them down to a few specific areas that appeal to them most. Then begin to look at the skill sets needed to succeed in those areas. An example is listed below.

Specific Passion in Athletic Category—Professional Athlete

+ *Understanding of contracts*—reading, mathematics and comprehension skills.
+ *Interviewing*—communication, reading and vocabulary skills.
+ *Autographs and possible books*—writing skills.
+ *Teamwork*—leadership and other soft skills

As you can see by this abbreviated version, a Passion Map™ is a powerful tool for helping students of color to connect their dreams to education. It shows them that if they have a certain passion and would like to spend their adult life succeeding in this area, there are certain skills they need to master now! Students who become aware of this information delivered in a fun and innovative way have a greater possibility of achieving success than those who do not get exposed to this information at all. The students begin to realize that their area of interest requires more to succeed than merely an interest in it. It takes the power of their current education to make it a reality.

4. Stay on the Course

A simplistic, yet powerful key, is staying on the chosen course until you see success. Commitment and consistency are key components to success. Many institutions start initiatives, but finish none. If you are going to motivate students of color, long-term motivational efforts are paramount. If not, you will find yourself going in circles, spiraling downward, and failing. A philosophy needs to be adopted that is serious about the process of encouraging students. Connecting dreams to education is key to success. Students who have and believe in a dream are students who will see the significance of their education. You and your school or organization can assist greatly in making their dream become reality.

Chapter Summary

Dr. Martin Luther King's famous speeches focus on a dream. Harriet Tubman placed her life on the line in order to see her dream of freedom for herself, her parents, and other slaves realized. Over the years, many people of color have battled in order to succeed in achieving and living the elusive American Dream. In this chapter I discussed a topic that is of utmost importance if we are ever going to close the achievement gap. If students of color do not begin to see the significance of an education relating to their dreams, where will we be 5, 10 or 15 years from now? At some point Black and Latino student success should become the norm, instead of an anomaly. If not now, when? Will students of color see their dream as an unreachable star, or as a realistic possibility? You possess one of the major ingredients to solidify their dream potential because you are around them for up to seven hours a day. It can be done!

Key 1

—Connecting Dreams To Education™ Highlights—

+ Understand the language of students to connect with them.

+ Know that history has not been kind to the development of our students' dreams.

+ Have structured rap sessions to discuss your students' aspirations.

+ Remember that a Passion Map™ is a powerful tool for taking common dream areas and connecting them to the power of education.

KEY 2

PASSION-IZING Your Delivery

Passion can be found in worship. For the last fifteen years I have attended church regularly, whether in my home church or that of a friend or colleague. A short time ago, a former colleague invited me to his church in St. Davids, PA. Although the congregation was somewhat reserved, the people were committed to their church and enjoyed their time together. The pastor was a very knowledgeable teacher who preached with nominal energy, followed his notes closely, and did not deviate too much from his style of preaching. The congregation was almost entirely Caucasian. By contrast, in my church, where the congregation is almost entirely African-American, from praise and worship to the altar call, there is high energy and high praise taking place. Members and visitors are very vocal in expressing their love for and thanks to God and are not self-conscious in doing so because this is typical in numerous Black and Latino churches. The pastors (regardless of ethnicity) are traditionally high energy, flamboyant yet astute in their presentations. Communal "amens" and a plethora of shouting and hand clapping are not unusual. This is the black experience.

Passion can also be found in celebrations. I marvel at how we celebrate the unity of family at our reunions. Lots of music, dancing and memorable, jubilant, loving conversations take place during these events. This is how we communicate. When we become sensitive to cultural differences, there are important considerations. The Black race is a high-energy race—we are very responsive to kinetic events, activities and individuals. When you work with youth from any culture, the way you deliver your message will be key to the success of your objectives. For students of color living in environments that typically communicate in high-energy fashion, it becomes difficult for them to sit through low-energy, non-interactive educational lectures (not impossible, but indeed a challenge.) In order to effectively reach the students, you must use creative, innovative delivery techniques. Traditional techniques need to be updated by progressive educators. In order to succeed, you must know your audience; this is one of the professional competencies of people in the motivational industry. It should become one for educators and mentors as well. You don't have to become a motivational speaker like myself or a high-energy preacher like Bishop T.D. Jakes, but if you acquire this unique attribute, you can meet cultural challenges when interacting with students of color. As all people have different learning styles, some cultures have an affinity for different teaching styles. This chapter will provide you with some important keys to consider when determining the style and delivery of your material. This information is based upon successful techniques used in our HYPE model.

Preparation & Delivery

Classrooms today are very diverse, populated by students of color, Caucasians, and other racial groups. Experience has taught me that in order to effectively connect with people—adults or youth—the speaker must *know* the audience. During my corporate years, I attended a class which focused on learning personality styles. At that time I was a newlywed experiencing challenges to understanding why my wife operated in the manner she did. Not until I sat in that class did I realize she and I operate based upon two widely varying styles. She has more of a driver personality, but I have more of an expressive one. I could not wait to get home and try my newfound communication techniques on my wife. To my surprise they worked! By getting to the point without excessive detail (as most expressive personalities do not), I established a newfound peace in my home, communicating in language that fit her style. What a powerful lesson! The facilitator had all of us captivated, showing us at the end of the session how he incorporated techniques in his delivery that touched on all of our styles. I then determined that his tailored techniques could effectively be adapted to working with different cultures as well, since many students are not connecting to merely one style of classroom delivery. Often inexperienced educators adopt styles which they find comfortable for themselves, but which may not suit their target audience. Effective teachers must consider the uniqueness and challenges of all their attendees, especially with the dramatic increase in classroom populations in recent years. Recognizing learning styles and personality styles are essential to teaching efficacy. The delivery must impact the thought processes of all of your students in order for them to remain excited about learning new and positive concepts and making significant paradigm shifts.

With the HYPE (Helping Youth Pursue Excellence) Program, we always consider our audience. Since we interact with and speak to a variety of races and cultures, we always take cultural differences into account during our preparation. There are several keys to making a delivery attractive to diverse groups.

Make It Interactive

My extensive travels have reconfirmed for me that the black culture is a high-energy one. It really does not matter what part of the world we come from—Jamaica, the Bahamas, England, the continent of Africa or any other part of the world. It was amazing to learn that although as a race we are in different parts of the world, we are very much the same in our attitudes and methods of operation. We prefer interaction when learning new things. Sitting in the classroom and reading out of a book does not impact us as much as taking the idea out of the book and expressing it through story or some other form of vernacular expression. My company uses a manual we developed to give the students to write down key points and use as a guide to follow along. During the program or speech, we engage students through interactive dialogue and assignments. The impact of this method has been so powerful that it has resulted in having our company deliver one of the most successful training programs relating to keeping kids throughout the state of Delaware enrolled in school. We have been contracted over the last five years to run a year round program for the state's Department of Labor. In the program we work with student grades 8-12 providing them with soft skills training using the HYPE Model. We also provide them with employment opportunities with non-profit organization during the summer months. One of the major successful keys of the program is the number of students who return to school. Our program has averaged 97% success over the last five years. None have dropped out, but a few have moved out of the area. If it were not for those who moved away, we would have a 100% success rate. I believe the reason for this success is the impact of our soft skills training coupled with the student relationships we have developed, because our entire curriculum is designed to be highly interactive. You may wonder how we do this in our classroom. It is all in the preparation, which takes much time and energy to complete. It sometimes meant dismantling the same approach which had been used for years and taking on a new paradigm. So when preparing *your* lesson plans, include personally developed or off-the-shelf material that is interactive. Read the trade journals of your associations to learn what others are doing successfully and adopt some of the same philosophies. Do search engine checks to find out what unique techniques are being used. The point I am making is "Think outside of the cycle"—the cycle of how you have always done things, especially if you are not having the success rates you are seeking. Interactivity can include, but is not limited to:

1. "rap" sessions
2. classroom meetings
3. group exercises
4. learning games and tools
5. personally developed material.

Interaction is a key component to motivating all students, particularly students of color. Using this teaching technique indicates that you are now student-centered in your approach, one which could make a remarkable difference in your students' perceptions and learning acuity.

Speak With Passion

I have worked in many classrooms in my years as a speaker and trainer, and I remember one year being contracted to conduct a series of motivational workshops for a 9th grade class at Mt. Pleasant High School in Wilmington, DE. Often I have been invited in to work with at-promise (I do not classify students as at-risk) youth and this school's invitation was no exception. However, there was a difference in how this class operated. I had no problems with the class; they showed the highest level of respect, and it was an absolute pleasure working with them. Normally I would credit my rapport building skills, connecting with the students, and other teaching techniques. Even though my methodology did help, the classroom environment was already established due to a teacher named Greg Shivery. All of his students loved him, showed him the ultimate respect, and responded to everything he had to say. He was an amazing educator who had a passion for teaching. You could hear it in his voice every time he spoke to the students. You could keenly sense that it was not simply a job for him: it was a mission. His love for the students permeated the classroom, and his delivery was genuine, impacting everyone in the room, including me. Because he was *living* his passion, he spoke with passion. You, too, can begin to see tremendous progress when you show what's in your heart in communicating with the students. When you teach, teach with passion, and show students you believe that they can do it. Your energy and vitality will be contagious. For example, when my son was in a Spanish immersion program, the founder of the school, Mercedes Alonzo exemplified this passion in the classroom daily. She energized the students: all of the 4, 5 and 6 year-olds were enthused to learn the language even though she did not teach Spanish in the classroom. She simply spoke it while teaching their K-1 curriculum. As a result, my son is not only fluent in Spanish, but he also loves his teacher. The school gets 100% parent support because all of the teachers exude passion when they teach. Display your passion for teaching, and begin to see the connection made, an important key to working with students of color.

Be Transparent

Students need to see you as imperfect, human. It is another way of connecting. All too often, young people are challenged by trying to meet the expectations of adults because most adults do a terrible job of sharing their own challenges faced both personally and professionally to get to their current positions in life. When adults try to paint flawless self-portraits, students often feel even more flawed. I tell my students everything from my trials faced as a child to some of the challenges and fears I face today, because

I want them to know that their problems do not have to limit their dreams. In my travels, I have found that the educators who relate some of their experiences with students in an educative way connect better with them. The students learn and become somewhat empathetic. If you are a Caucasian educator teaching Black or Latino students, this technique is of greater significance. I often hear students say, "They can't relate to me because they never lived my life." But, by showing the students that you had to overcome obstacles to get to where you are today, they will begin to see you as truly human. Don't hide your life inside of a vault, share your experiences in such a way that your students begin to see you as a model of perseverance. By adding this to your delivery, you will begin to see the students' attitudes change towards you and your educational message. One story I often share with the students is about my upbringing: how my father left home shortly after I was born; how my mother with only an 8th grade education raised two boys on welfare for many years. Then I share how she returned to school to earn her GED and went on to business school to successfully earn a secretarial certificate. From that point, she landed a job with a small airline called Allegheny, which today is known as US Air, a very resilient company. This personal story demonstrates to students that this Coach D understands the issues that many of them face and that they can win regardless. Just as my mother did, they can maximize their educational opportunities and go for the gold. Her decision changed my expectation for success in life. Be transparent; show your kids you are human just as they are.

Listen

Many deliveries are monologues—one-way conversations. Some speakers have this problem on the dais, failing to realize that no matter the size of the crowd, people need to be heard. Whenever

I present a motivational speech (whether it is to 50 or 5000 people), I ask questions constantly to get their responses. Frequently I can use their comments for speech material, so this shows the audience that I am listening. On numerous occasions, I have randomly telephoned various event attendees just to get industry-specific or school-specific information to help me better connect with my clients when I'm on the stage. In many circumstances, listening is more powerful than speaking. In the school systems across America I find that too many educators seem not to value youth input, so they never ask for it. My company has done just the opposite and continues to experience tremendous success. By listening to what students are saying, you can learn keys to helping them improve in the classroom. You can accomplish this by the use of surveys, one-on-one meetings and other methodologies which you and your team may develop. The best way is by the classroom meetings mentioned earlier in the chapter. Giving students a chance to talk in a non-threatening, well-prepared classroom setting affords them the venue to share what's on their heart. This information is invaluable in the delivery of your educational message. Described below is an exercise to help you in the information gathering process.

Classroom Information Gathering

In this exercise you are going to meet with the students and allow them to express their thoughts about the classroom, school and education as a whole. By doing this for ½ hour, every three to four weeks, you can gather valuable information that can help in your quest to inspire students. If you are having problems currently in the classroom, you may get some harsh responses initially, but by working on improving your relationship with the students employing some of the techniques mentioned in this book, you will eventually begin to see your students improve. Take a moment and ask your students to fill out this informal survey:

Question 1. What do you like about being
a student in this class?

Question 2. What do you dislike about being
a student in this class?

Question 3. What is one thing I can change in order
to make this the best classroom environment for you?

Question 4. What is one thing that you can change
in order to make this the best classroom environment?

Question 5. In what way can we work together
so that everyone in the classroom can succeed?

The purpose of this exercise is to get students to provide you with information that can assist in making the classroom an invaluable experience. It allows students of color especially to express what is really on their hearts, while it allows you to have a greater understanding of their hearts and minds. If properly applied, this information can add to your effective classroom delivery.

Please keep in mind that I am sharing ideas upon which you can *build.* Find creative ways to customize the ideas to your class situation.

Chapter Summary

In order to bring energy to your delivery, you need to understand your clientele. I say clientele because without students, we all would be unemployed; they are indeed the clients of the school system. Companies worldwide conduct prodigious amounts of research to determine the best ways to engage and persuade their clients. MTV, Nike and other companies spend countless hours in malls, at theme parks and other places trying to understand the mind set of their client base. The school system could learn from their strategies. We in many ways need to take on the mindset of the corporations. I am not talking about analyzing the negative reports relating to the increase of students of color in special education; we can become proactive so that the numbers in this category can steadily decrease until zero is the norm. I believe this has to be done on a class-to-class basis at the grass roots level. Your delivery and understanding of your students' cultures and styles will go a very long way in closing the achievement gap. Our nation's future depends on it.

Key 2

—PASSION-IZING Your Delivery Highlights—

+ People of color are high energy and are accustomed to high-energy interaction.

+ Your material delivery should consider the cultural differences in your students.

+ When sharing personal information, share it with passion. Demonstrate to students that you believe in yourself despite your flaws, and especially in them.

+ Meet with your students often in an effort to understand their thoughts and challenges.

+ The problems faced in the educational community will be fixed at the grass roots level.

KEY **3**

Developing Student Councils

Several years ago when we first started our company we realized the value of youth input as it related to academic and personal success, so we regularly shared with city governments, state government and school districts that programs needed to be developed which engaged students in the problem solving and future development process. Back then, however, people did not buy into our vision. Somewhat discouraged, I called on people who I met just to discuss my thoughts and to get some feedback. A man named Bob Strong who supervised School-to-Work for the Department of Education encouraged me to hang in there. He believed that my ideas made sense, and that one day people would listen. Our company was and is passionate about councils being developed that will help students work with fellow students, educators and parents in order to develop their own self esteem through self-determination. We believed that if students could come together in a structured format to discuss problems and create innovative solutions, they could also become a part of the change process and be leaders in the movement towards positive change. They would also take ownership for their future outcomes, we determined. As a result of not giving up on the vision, today we have formed a plethora of councils for city and county governments, school districts and departments of education. One mayor even proclaimed a day in his city for a youth leadership institute we established there. Many of the councils which we have developed are heavily populated by students of color. The power of this plan has been amazing! Many students who people said would never work together now work in harmony on various projects. They select council presidents and boards, and these councils have dispelled the myth that kids cannot think critically. If given the guidance and the opportunity, they can come up with answers that would dazzle the mind of any adult. Council development is a great motivator for students of color because it gives them an outlet to express themselves and helps them to feel that their input is important. The goal of this chapter is to discuss the importance of council development—in particular, its benefits to students of color. Later, I will discuss the power of educator councils as well.

The Power of Councils

The whole council concept as you know is not a new one: city councils help to manage the affairs of a metropolitan area, and county councils manage the affairs of an entire county. In their meetings, council members analyze the decisions that need to be made for their city or county to come up with the best solutions based upon the needs of their constituents. A lot of negotiating occurs, many problems are discussed, and issues are resolved. Effective meetings are results oriented and focused. Developing a youth council would empower young people in your school or organization to get involved with the decision making process. Participation teaches them critical negotiating skills, communication skills, rapport building skills and project management skills. The most important aspect of the council from my perspective is the sense of ownership taken by the students. Most of the councils we have helped to develop have resulted in students controlling the outcomes of the council, thus developing the critical skill of taking control of their own outcomes in life. One of the fundamental successes behind our HYPE program is from day one we engage the students and always value their opinions. We do not treat them like drones which lack the ability to think for themselves; we treat them like young people who have exceptional minds if given the chance to maximize them fully. Council development is one critical factor in achieving this goal. The greatest strength of the motivational effect of student councils is that they are self-motivating. Through the process of analysis, synthesis and judgment (according to Dr. Benjamin Bloom and our own empirical studies), students become self motivated to achieve the goals of the council as well as their own personal goals.

The Significance To Students Of Color

Of all of the activities in which we are involved in the HYPE Program, we see the greatest level of synergy and energy displayed when students are selected to be a part of something positive. A number of programs for which we have been contracted are somewhat challenging due to students' personal perceptions such as the perception that they as students need this person to motivate them beyond their challenges (even though they did not ask for him). I have found that motivation is at its highest when students are selected to be part of something special, something that is part of a decision-making process. This plays a significant role in motivating students of color. Often they feel that people do not value their opinion and deal with them based upon preconceived notions. Getting them involved in the developmental process of academic, social and personal success, often, for the first time gives them the opportunity to perceive themselves in a better light. Recently, I was honored by a group of students who comprise the State of Delaware's Special Education Youth Advisory Council. It was one of those teary-eyed moments, if you know what I mean. I received many praises and comments from the students and advisors, and their heartfelt comments were especially touching. One parent e-mailed me after the event thanking me for helping to turn her son's life around. The council had the student seeing himself in a new way. Several of the advisors announced that their students were on fire to make a difference. These comments were so powerful because I simply allowed the students, through the development of the council, to use their intellectual skills that in many instances were merely lying dormant. Their amazing abilities were inside them all along, so it only took the formation of the council to awaken them. This is a powerful principle in motivating students of color. According to the Bloom model, the problem has been that many people do not allow the students to think at the highest levels by simply not using creative techniques such as council development. Too frequently there are erroneous assumptions with which people live and refuse to move beyond. A school or classroom council can be a way to elevate students to another level of interpersonal motivation.

How Are They Formed?

Our company spends countless hours consulting organizations on this process. It is not a frivolous undertaking, especially if you are looking for seriously positive results. There are several key factors to consider, however.

1. How Many Students Will Be On The Council?

I have found that too many students make it ineffective, but with just a few students you will see greater success. Usually up to 15 students is a good number because 20 and higher make success rates more difficult. Having worked with numerous organizations desiring to have fifty or more students involved, I immediately told them that the program would not work because a smaller number of students is needed at the beginning, in order to work efficiently and quantify success.

2. Who Should Be On The Council?

This is another area of contention with people. Many people want to start their first councils with extremely difficult students, and frown when I tell them this is a recipe for disaster. There needs to be a mixture of students on the council. In the first endeavor, students should go through an interview process to be a part of the council. Students should not be selected based upon your relationship with them, or your perception that this is going to immediately fix a problematic child. Instead, select a diverse group to serve on the council. By effectively interviewing the students, and making the interview the selection criteria, you will find students who will become more committed to your endeavor. Once the students are selected, have them sign a contract (non-binding, of course) that they will stay committed to the council and work diligently when involved. This is a key to long-term success.

3. What Goals Should You Set?

The council goals will depend on what type of council you are looking to develop. To establish a leadership council, set goals that will exemplify leadership characteristics. To establish an advisory council, outline goals that will center on providing advice which pertains to the academic success of the classroom, school, or community. Determine program-specific goals such as the number of meetings, frequency, length, and order of meetings, incentives etc. Your council process must be well thought out if it is to be successful and regenerative.

4. Should There Be Standards?

Standards are extremely beneficial. We have set everything from academic standards to community services standards. Standards are part of the admission process. The standards should be within reason and necessary to help raise the students' personal bar. The students need to stretch beyond themselves in order for the council process to succeed. The goal is to have them consider it an honor to participate, and a commitment for them to maintain.

5. What Should Adult Advisors Consider?

The first thing to consider is your motivation for establishing the council. If the motivation is to guide the students towards personal and academic success, then go for it. If the motivation is to help students begin to think at the higher levels, go for it. If the motivation is encourage motivate students of color to overcome barriers to success, go for it. But if you see it as an extra responsibility and something not internally motivating, do not go for it. In all of the councils we have helped to establish, one common success factor has been the organization's on-going commitment. In order to make the council concept succeed you must:

1. involve people who are committed
    to making it a success;
2. be willing to stay in it for the long haul;
3. love young people unconditionally;
4. provide direction and focus to the students.
    They need direction from the adult advisors.

The Power of Responsibility

Of all the things we do as a company I am convinced that council development is one of the most significant. If you seek to empower and motivate your students of color, this is an invaluable tool. Obviously, the councils in most schools will not consist only of students of color, but the impact upon students of color will be quite valuable. By engaging them in the process of taking responsibility on this level, they will begin to see themselves in a more positive way. Responsibility is a great tool for internal change and stability. As children, my brother and I were given household responsibilities, but many of our friends did not have the same responsibilities, so I remember complaining that my friends could spend more time doing other things. My mother would always reply, "I am not their mother, and you *will* take care of your chores." I was annoyed by her remarks then, but as a man I am grateful for her steadfastness. Because of her persistence, I have become a responsible husband, father and business owner. Certainly, my mother's commitment to responsibility helped me become the man I am today. Further, I am convinced that having young people take responsibility will help them to develop the skills to make sound choices about their future. This is the real power of a council: when developed properly, it can change the mindset of students, schools, or organizations within a short period of time.

Educator Peer Councils

Another type of council that can be beneficial in your quest to motivate students is the development of educator councils in your school or school district. Educator councils may consist of counselors, teachers, school psychologists and administrators and are formed to focus on personal motivation strategic meetings as well as to discuss tools for motivating students of colors. Monthly meetings to discuss strategies for staying personally motivated on the job can be beneficial to professional and personal growth. During the meetings you can include discussion questions such as those listed below.

1. What are tools we can develop to remain personally motivated on the job?
2. What are some creative tools we can develop or use to motivate our students of color regularly?
3. How can we hold ourselves accountable as a school to this initiative?
4. What is working, what is not?
5. What is our philosophy regarding this initiative?

As with other concepts shared in this book, commitment is one of the keys to success when establishing educator councils. Only recruit people who are willing to commit and take responsibility for the success of motivating students of color. You *can* make it happen! I am confident in your ability to close the gap in your school.

Chapter Summary

It is important to mention at this juncture that we are sharing a plethora of ideas stemming from the success of our HYPE model. Although not all of the concepts will be the perfect fit for you, your school, or district, when you find ideas that inspire, use them enthusiastically. The council idea is a great idea for most schools and classrooms where there are committed groups of people. What I am encouraging throughout this book is to try new and innovative ideas for motivating students of color. Although this is the primary focus, these ideas will benefit all students. If there are any specific questions you may have regarding our techniques, please contact my office or e-mail your question. Our goal is to see you succeed in achieving your goal of student motivation.

Key 3

Developing Student Councils—Highlights

+ Councils are an integral tool for helping students to become self-motivated.

+ Councils provide opportunities for students to take personal responsibility.

+ In order for councils to succeed, adults and students must be committed.

+ Specific goals must be established in writing, employing input from students.

+ Educator councils are beneficial for personal and student motivation.

KEY4

Purging The Past

Let me preface this chapter by saying that the information we are about to share is for all people, not limited to people of color. The purpose of this chapter is not to understand your students, but for you to understand yourself. We all have been influenced by a past that causes us to make decision on how we:

- ✦ Raise our children
- ✦ See the world and its inhabitants
- ✦ Operate in relationships
- ✦ Dress
- ✦ Pursue careers
- ✦ Do much more!

I have found that we are all products of life's influences. People are usually influenced by a few factors, not the least of which include:

- ✦ Heredity
- ✦ Relationships
- ✦ Environment

Many times the attitudes of educators, administrators, principals and others are influenced by these factors. The level of determination in a student is also influenced by these factors. The expected outcomes of an organizational leader, many times are influenced by these factors. In order to change an environment toward producing significant and positive goals, we must identify interpersonal characteristics derived from negative personal experiences, and begin the process of purging them. Throughout years of working with people, we have identified three factors that shape the decisions of people worldwide:

+ Generational Transfers
+ Negative Mental Habits
+ Access To Knowledge

Generational Transfers

Generational transfers are defined as individuals taking on the traits of their parents and fore parents. This is very evident in economically challenged populations where many individuals are second and third generation in this category. For persons born in a progressive environment, it may seem as though these people are lazy and don't want anything out of life, yet, this is not a fair assessment because it is quite obvious that these economically challenged individuals have adapted to a lifestyle that is very normal to them; their mothers, fathers, and in many cases, grandparents and even great grandparents lived in similar situations. So the norm has been to mirror the image most familiar to them. If not properly trained to aspire higher, in many cases over a period of years, these persons will simply pass this inherited mindset to the next generation. This same pattern of mirroring is also true of most people who were born in progressive households; they adapt to the mindset of *their* parents and fore parents. My son Darrell is already interested in working with his dad. He has seen the image of his father encouraging and energizing people worldwide, and he wants to do the same thing. His aspirations have been shaped by the image that his mother and I have shaped for him. Pastor Ted Tripp calls it "Shaping Influences." In both case scenarios there are exceptions, however it most cases both ring true. We are aware of Pavlov's Classical Conditioning, so in some ways we, too, like the animals which responded to the bell, are shaped to an extent by the power of influence. This is evident in areas besides socio-economics; it is also evident in our racial beliefs, communication styles, traditions, thoughts, the clothes we wear, our hairstyles and the like. As it relates to working with students of color, many of our perspectives come from communications and perceptions shaped by our family and community. Our upbringing impacts the way we see people. This is a challenge even in today's school system.

The problem with many of these transfers is that we think *we* control *them* but in reality, *they* control *us*. Some people cannot explain why they see people in the way they do, but chances are if you were to look at their lives from a historical perspective chances are it was due to family acceptance of a stereotype. It may have been the topic of discussion at a dinner table or a discussion with friends. In order to change this disabler, people must purge the old mindset and establish a new one. If this is never dealt with, the stagnant way of thinking is simply passed on. I encourage everyone reading this book to answer a few simple questions:

1. Why do you *think* that you think the way you do?
2. What incorrect perception of people have you adopted that may be generational?
3. What must you do to change this perception?
4. What will be the benefits to you and others as a result?
5. As an educator, what will be the benefit to your student and school environment by making this change?

Negative Mental Habits

Negative mental habits in many cases are derived from a life saturated with pessimism, and examples of uncontrolled behavior due in many cases to environment, from generational transfers. The problem deriving from these bad mental habits is that they are very hard to break. Once they have penetrated the mind of the individual they build a habitation there. In some cases psychological help may be needed; however, in most cases, proper training over long periods of time coupled with life mentors can improve the situation. I remember a circumstance in which one individual provided a negative example for many of the young men in his family. As a result of his influence, many of them walked like him, talked like him and acted like him. Most of those who followed his lead ended up unfortunately in jail or in the grave. The mental pictures that were placed in their heads were ones of uncontrolled, unacceptable behavior. They developed mental habits and life patterns based upon their reverence for his every move. I have counseled countless young men who have undergone similar experiences. One young man we worked with was disruptive in his classroom. He was not a violent young man by any stretch of the imagination; however, he was a challenge to his teachers. Most of them came to the conclusion that he was simply a difficult to serve student. After one counseling session—one in which I listened more than talked—I found out that he was exhibiting this behavior because the father had been in prison all of the young man's life, this young man expected to share his father's fate. His image was crafted by the vision of his father in prison, so his mental habits were developed around this image. After I spent additional time with the young man he turned things around. I supplied him with a barrage of purpose-building exercises to help him paint a positive picture of his future. His teacher contacted me a few weeks later and stated, "I have a new student in my classroom. This young man has made a 180 degree turnaround."

Some of the better-known negative mental habits are:

1. Pessimism
2. Sarcasm
3. Low self-esteem
4. Procrastination
5. Making excuses
6. Disrespect
7. Lack of desire
8. Blaming others for shortcomings
9. Irresponsible behavior
10. Lack of focus

On one particular occasion, I conducted an in-service seminar for a group of special education teachers. The focus of the workshop was to address student motivation and to help them overcome interpersonal barriers to student progress. I posed two questions: "What negative perceptions have you encapsulated about certain students? In what ways are these thoughts holding you back from helping them reaching their true potential?" One bold Caucasian teacher, in tears, raised her hand. She admitted sadly, "Coach, all of my life I have had the perception that young African-American males are all violent, disrespectful and connected to street life. Even when one was easy to work with, I still sort of looked at the rest of them in this manner because this is how I have historically looked at them. This was my mindset. Today, this mindset will change." The group gave her a hug, and I did as well. I told her that I was proud of her for being honest. "If we could get people all over the country to do what you just did, we can significantly impact the potential in our classrooms." Her story shows that we do not have to be trapped in old thought patterns. We, in many cases, are only one decision away from changing our paradigms.

Access To Knowledge

Sometimes individuals feel overwhelmed and trapped by a situation or by life's circumstances because of a lack of knowledge. Often, they meander through life wondering what it all means. Because of comfortable relationships with certain people, some of these individuals will go to them for insight, but often the people from whom they seek assistance are in the same boat or worse. The advice they receive usually may provide comfort, but do not provide insight since the ones to whom they send out distress signals are people who are themselves in distress. So by not obtaining the proper knowledge, they remain trapped. In order to improve, access to knowledge and information is key. If the level of knowledge a person has is limited to his or her environment only, he or she may resolve that this is the limit of his or her world. When I was conducting a youth conference focusing on soft-skills in the workplace, one of the young men we selected to participate in the exercise seemed extremely nervous. We were going to ask him question about keys to success in the workplace. He leaned over to one of our staff members and said, "Miss, I live in the hood! We don't know anything about keys to success in the workplace." She assured him that Coach D would make it fun and interactive. His paradigm was that all people in the neighbor*hood* were limited as it related to knowledge of the workplace. Countless people have succeeded who were from the *hood*, but had a positive mindset. I am one of them. The young man's knowledge was limited due to his lack of exposure to information. But knowledge coupled with proper application can improve a person's life scenario. Reading books, listening to tapes, and conversing with successful people reveal information that can create a new destiny for those seeking a better way of life. Unfortunately many people do not have access to this information, so they limit their possibilities—sometimes indefinitely.

Take advantage of the mind-changing information that is available. I have spent a number of years reading books and listening to tapes on change. I realize that I cannot get new results in my life if I continue to think in the old manner. Many times one piece of solid information can change a life forever. So go for it! Your students are depending on you.

The Purging Process

Change is a key factor for success but one that is rarely embraced. In order to significantly impact the educational performance of students of color, people who work with the students on a daily basis must purge the interpersonal characteristics that hinder their ability to see the students' true potential. *It is humanly impossible* to *create positive outcomes with a negative mindset.* We must also come up with ways to purge the past mental strongholds developed by the students themselves. There must be programs developed by the schools and organizations that can help the students to see for themselves what they can become, not what they are perceived to be or what they have been. I recently visited one of the most amazing Charter Schools in the country: The Mathematics, Civics and Sciences Charter School in Philadelphia, PA. The school is headed by Ms. Veronica Joyner, Founder and CAO, a woman who is passionate about educating students of color. Ms. Joyner and I started the day by visiting the first grade in the school (the school serves grades 1-12, enrolls over 1000 students, and has a waiting list of more than 5000 students). The students all stood up and greeted their principal, who they all love dearly, and me. They shared the vision of the school, the school's history, and Ms. Joyner's mission to build future leaders, all in unison. She called out the names of students to have them respond to various math, science or grammar questions. Ninety nine percent of their answers were correct! This happened again when we visited the second grade, third grade, fourth grade, all the way up to the seniors. As we walked through the halls I noticed the pictures of great black historians, athletes, actors, entertainers, and other public figures. She was shaping the image of what the children could become. Most of the kids came from public schools of Philadelphia and were considered at-risk and low income, but Ms. Joyner's method of education, coupled with old-fashioned love and care, purged their system of impossibilities.

Two girls approached us during my tour and described a conflict that was developing. Ms. Joyner pulled both girls aside, placed them in a study room, and advised them to resolve the conflict. We continued with the tour. Less than twenty minutes later we went back to the room to see that the girls were laughing and communicating with each other respectfully. I asked her how she did that. She told me that all students have to go through conflict resolution and peer mediation training to learn to resolve conflicts amongst themselves. Amazing! I sat there with my mouth wide open in awe. This woman, whose school is only five years old, has been able to create a model of success unlike any other place I have visited. More than 92 % of her seniors were admitted to college, most receiving scholarships. This school from my perspective exemplifies everything I will share in this book. Paul Vallas, CEO of the Philadelphia School System affirms her success in this way: "I consider her school one of the best I have visited to date and invited her to serve as a role model for other charter schools in the district." Hats off to you, Ms. Joyner, for believing the HYPE!

This story proves that the image you see will be the image that will succeed. School systems across this country and worldwide must adopt the same attitude adopted by Ms. Joyner. For many, however, it means getting a fresh perspective on the possibilities for our students. It is time to purge the old and bring in the new. For those who work with the students—teacher, principals, counselors and others—listed below are ways to purge old internal paradigms:

1. Be honest. If you are challenged with generational transfers, habits or knowledge, be honest with yourself.
2. Seek help. It may mean taking a cultural sensitivity course or finding a mentor who exemplifies the behavior you would like to achieve.
3. Act as if the student is your own child. How would you treat him or her? Would you be more compassionate, would your commitment intensify?
4. Deal with weaknesses systematically. Identify common problems for individuals in your schools and develop support structures to help those who need assistance.
5. Don't give up until change takes place. Realize that you entered into teaching for your love of educating students, and all children need to be loved and respected in the same manner.

I have been pleading with school and school districts to make interpersonal change a priority. We keep going in circles because organizations focus on building programs instead of building people. *A new program will never work with an old mindset.* Motivating students of color and all students is dependent upon changing stakeholders as well as systems. If we are truly going achieve No Child Left Behind, we must also leave behind old dispositions and attitudes.

Key 4

—Purging the Past Highlights—

+ We are all, in some way, impacted by generational transfers.

+ Our perceptions of others can easily become our reality.

+ We must first recognize that the problem exists before change can occur.

+ We can learn from the actions and attitude of Mrs. Veronica Joyner.

+ If we are going to have no child left behind, we must leave our negative perceptions behind.

Key5

Understanding the Changing Times

I remember working with a group of students in the development of a youth council. I always enjoy this interaction with students, watching them become leaders right before my eyes. In a conversation I was having with a young man about parental discipline, he asked "You lived in the day when parents would really discipline you for doing something wrong didn't you?" "Yes, "I replied. He then asked "I bet you had to be in the house early too, didn't you?" Again, I answered "Yes, and look at the result." He exclaimed, "Boy, I could never have lived in those days!" Please keep in mind that these were not the days of the dinosaur; I'm talking about the seventies and eighties when I was growing up. Who would have imagined in such short period, discipline would have declined in such a dramatic fashion? As I will repeatedly say in this book, I am not just talking about students of color, but this phenomenon is impacting all young people. The thought of school violence was virtually unheard of twenty years ago. Today there are youth in suburbia who have committed crimes too heartbreaking to mention in this book. What is happening to the lives of our young people that we as educators need to think about? What is impacting the thought patterns of today's youth that we need to consider? Listed below are a few areas I believe have to be researched and considered when looking at the process of positive motivation of youth.

The Family Structure

Do you remember the show *Happy Days*? The show featured a family named the Cunninghams. Ritchie Cunningham, (played by Ron Howard, now a famous producer) was the star of the show: a teenager with good morals and a generous heart. The co-star was a cool guy named "The Fonz" (played by Henry Winkler, now also an acclaimed producer). What I remember most about the show is that there was always a positive, a happy ending. The Fonz was always loved and respected by Ritchie's family. Although Ritchie and his little sister Joni would have their fair share of problems, they would fall back on their strong, moral upbringing in times of trouble. They would eat dinner together, discuss family issues together, and discuss their futures together. Wouldn't it be great if we lived in the world of *Happy Days?*

Times have changed and so has the family structure. Back then, traditional families consisted of a mother and a father. Today, there is a plethora of households: single parent, latch key, gay and lesbian, grandparent only, and blended. Families once considered non-traditional are today more the rule than the exception. This poses a new set of circumstances that all educators need to consider. The demographic element most impacting students of color is the single parent household. In the state where I live, the percentage of African-American single parent households is twofold that of Caucasian single parent households.

What are the challenges of being raised in a single parent household? We'll I can share this from personal experience because my mother was a single parent. Four of the challenges are parental fatigue, lack of effective male role models, depression, and maintaining a positive family value system.

A. Parental Fatigue

Many times we become extremely critical of parents who are raising children by themselves. Imagine having to deal all alone with the following:

- cooking dinner
- washing clothes
- working outside the home
- taking children to the doctor
- paying the bills
- handling family emergencies
- teaching a son about manhood
- teaching a daughter how to become a respectable woman
- visiting the children's school
- attending school events
- staying motivated and determined around the children

Imagine doing this and much more without a supportive spouse! I suspect that some of you are saying "We'll I did it, why can't they?" My response to you is "If life were that simple, we would all be saints living in a perfect world." Some people, for whatever reason, have the drive and determination to excel no matter what the situation, while others do not have it that easy. I find that many single parents are physically tired. When I look at the amount of work both my wife and I invest into being effective as parents coupled with our many other responsibilities, it's quite difficult to picture one person undertaking the work of two without relief. In trying to comprehend the changing times, please realize that often, single parents have more responsibilities than they can handle comfortably. If you have students in your classroom who come from single parent households, they may be experiencing challenges not faced by students from two parent households. Again, I am not saying that single parents cannot raise a morally sound, driven and ambitious children. What I am saying is that this is an issue for you to consider when attempting to bridge the gap in regards to motivating today's students. These parents may be so physically and mentally exhausted that they find parental involvement a significant challenge.

B. Lack of Effective Male Role Models

In my experiences growing up, it was normal to see single parent households, and the majority of them were run by women. In my family, the dominant forces were my mother and two grandmothers. There just were no solid male role models—period! As a child, I was told by various "manhood experts" (smile) that manhood was based upon the number of female conquests you made, or in the best scenario, your level of employment. No one ever explained to me then that none of these examples really defined manhood. Even today, many of our young men are confused about manhood. In many African cultures and in the Jewish tradition, there are ceremonies that celebrate manhood, and the young men are supported through the process. Yet for most young men of color, it is hit or miss. There is pressure on the females of the community to provide insight into what a real man consists of. I recall that my mother would do things like wrestle with us, attempt to play sports with us and take us to events in which she assumed young men would be interested. Because my brother and I lacked a positive male role model, she had to become a mother and a father. This is still far too prevalent in today's society and poses another major problem.

C. Depression

I often hear the question, "Why are those parents not involved in their children's education? Why do they not attend the regular meetings we schedule?" One of the reasons could simply be depression. As aforementioned, among the many challenges faced by single parents, may very well be overcoming a sense of hopelessness, especially if the parent has to raise several children alone. I have commonly witnessed parents who exhibit symptoms of depression but who deny they exist. This is frequently a problem that goes undiagnosed in many parents.

While single parenting is a significant issue nationwide, it is of epidemic proportion in minority communities. This simply illuminates a problem that is pervasive today, and it is important in the education community to explore ways to handle this problem. Some strategies will be shared in the book to increase parental involvement.

D. Family Value System

In my household values reign supreme: we are committed to rearing morally, educationally and spiritually sound children. Today we have tools that make the process easier for us than it was for my mother. As I was growing up, family values were imparted regularly at the dinner table, as well as during family picnics and gatherings. Today, in the fast food generation, family interaction at mealtime is on a steep decline. It seems that now, morally, anything goes; and this mindset is seriously impacting our youth. All too frequently, family values are simply no longer paramount. For example, within the last year several couples my wife and I know have divorced. In every case, the divorcees had small children, and in most of those cases, the children were not even considered. Family unity and determination to stay committed to their wedding vows were not priorities. Thus their children will be torn between two parents because the model of family was discarded, and selfish personal feelings dominated. All couples have challenges, yet the family should be so important that they work through those challenges for the sake of the family. Preservation of the family unit should be important enough to fight for. Exceptions to the rule include cases of infidelity, spousal abuse or child abuse. Children need to receive shared values from both parents. Unfortunately, we do not see enough of this today.

Television, Music, and Print Media

Television in particular has the most significant impact on the thinking of a society. Consider the success of the show *American Idol*. This year alone, over 65 million people voted in the finals, which means that almost twenty five percent of the USA populace was glued to their television sets. As educators, parents, and mentors of youth, we need to be current and aware of the influences of the media on our children because it has, without question, a major impact upon the mindsets of our modern youth.

In the seventies there was a series of shows like *Happy Days* to which I referred in the last segment; even the game shows were wholesome and respectful. Popular music of that era was the same way. There were only rare cases in which songs did not echo the morality and standards of the time. Such is not the case today; there is virtually no censure of what a person can explicitly sing in a song, say in an interview, or write in a printed article! Recently I was viewing an evening talk show during which a famous musician and his mother were being interviewed. While they were walking around his old neighborhood, reflecting on his past, the interviewer asked the artist's mother "What is one thing you would like to see your son change in his music?" She responded, "I wish he would eliminate the profanity he uses."

Her famous son reacted by blurting out a stream of obscenities. What influence might this have had on his impressionable fans? This is what we have to contend with. It would be so rewarding if the positive aspects of youth were illuminated over the negative in the media, the problem is that *positive* does not sell records, *positive* does not sell prime time television, *positive* does not sell newspapers, *positive* does not sell magazines, nor does *positive* sell tabloids.

Minimal Expectations

Another challenge today based upon experience working with youth is minimal expectations. An example of this is an event that took place in the middle of a school rally I was conducting. I had several of the youth come on stage to share their dreams with the audience. The activity was going quite well until right in the middle of the event the principal walked up to the stage and gave me the "cut" sign. Although confused, I complied by ending the activity. This had never happened to me during an assembly. After the event we had a brief conversation about the incident, and he stated that one of the young ladies I selected was mentally disabled, so he signaled "cut" to protect her. When I asked him, "If a person is mentally disabled, does this mean that he or she has a difficult time understanding his or her actions or what is being communicated?" His response was affirmative. I informed him that although there were close to 500 kids in the auditorium, she was one of only seven who had the confidence to raise her hand and volunteer to participate. From my perspective, she understood clearly what she was getting into and had the confidence to try. He responded by saying, "It was my job to stop her." In the State of Delaware, I have helped the Department of Education to establish one of the nation's first Special Education Students and Students with Disabilities Youth Leadership Advisory Councils.

One thing we never considered from day one was the thought: they can't. Our philosophy is "If they have the confidence to try, let them try!" This is self-determination at its best. As a result of this effort, we have established a statewide initiative with student clubs in many of the schools; and the students, with the assistance of an adult liaison, are involved in a multitude of activities that many people once believed impossible for children with disabilities. It is only impossible if someone imposes a limit on the students' potential. Many young people of color experience low expectations. Often people do not expect much out of them, so they are encouraged to make only a barely minimal effort. This does not help the students; this cripples them. All students need to be encouraged and challenged to step out of their comfort zone, so challenge them to do and become their very best.

Chapter Conclusion

Since the seventies, times may have changed, values may have changed, television programs may have changed and attitudes may have changed. Yet I do not believe that the values upon which we have built this country must change. We can still educate our children with excellence in mind, work together to provide a high quality of education for all students in the nation, overcome the color barrier, and see student success as the norm. We can motivate our children to success by showing love and consideration to all of humanity. To do this, we must understand the changing times but still hold onto those positive values which form the foundation of our great nation.

Key 5

Understanding the Changing Times—Highlights

+ Times may have changed; however, certain positive values do not have to change.

+ It is necessary to show compassion when working with students of single parent households.

+ The media too frequently has a negative effect on the values of today's children.

+ We have to understand the times in order to create strategies for successfully working with today's youth.

Key 6

Bridging The Parent Gap

Insufficient parental support is unquestionably a gap which educators and mentors must close in order to improve the chances for student success. I remember being invited to an open-house program at a local high school where the staff was diligent in preparing for the parents. Student work was prominently displayed, the teachers were excited, and the principal went out of his way to make certain that parents would feel welcome. Despite all of the hard work and preparation, only four parents showed up; yet there were close to 300 students enrolled. This occurrence supports the belief that we have a major problem when it comes to parental involvement in the school systems today. This chapter will provide some insight into why there have been challenges in motivating parents of color by discussing the problem and providing possible and probable solutions. As started earlier, these are strategic ideas for you to consider and assess. The key to overall success is your ability to evaluate and determine the best options based upon your organization's circumstances.

PROBLEM #1—A High Number of Single Parent Households

This challenge has been discussed in detail in the earlier chapters. Many schools face difficulty getting single parents to participate in activities that are important to their children's success in school because there are numerous daily challenges faced by parents today. For them, working outside of the home, cleaning clothes, preparing dinner, managing limited finances, and putting out domestic "fires" are just a part of the daily routine.

Parents in this category may not be only low-income; in fact, they could be middle-class or even well-to-do. The challenge for them remains the responsibility of running a household single-handedly. I have counseled many such parents who often feel compelled to see their children achieve the level of success they themselves have achieved, and their guilt comes from not having enough time to become involved in their children's activities.

There is another category of single parents: those who do not have all of the responsibilities aforementioned, but who do not make their children's education a priority. These parents do not feel challenged because they fail to see a problem with their lack of a sense of responsibility, and their neighbors share their apathy. (I know this from personal experiences.) The handling of their challenges is more complex than the category of the hard working single parents who have time management issues. Parents who find comfort in apathy require assistance in establishing and rearranging their priorities. No matter what category, single parenting challenges households of color; therefore, educators need to be particularly innovative in bridging the connection gap with these parents.

Possible Solutions

A. Establish Parent-Student Goals That Can Be Supported By the School

Goals positioned correctively can have a profound effect on overall success. While helping to construct the special education council in Delaware, we found it difficult to involve parents with their children's IEP's. One young lady who was a part of the group encouraged her mother to get involved. She also helped to construct the plan based upon the goals she realized were attainable. So successful was she at doing this, coupled with her activities on council (with the direction of her school coordinator Becky Kelly), that she was invited to speak at conferences throughout the nation about this concept. Additionally, she was extremely successful in school despite having various learning disabilities. Her mother was involved with the goals that were established for the year, so this had significant impact upon her academic achievement.

By engaging parents in the goal-setting process, educators have a legal document to encourage family participation. This document needs to be agreed upon near the beginning of the year so that the goals can be measured throughout the school term. If a child is non-compliant, parents can be contacted to discuss some methods of amelioration, another critical factor that must be established right away. The parents need to be reached to discuss the non-compliance, as well as be applauded for the successes. Such contact should be arranged by the teacher, school counselor or other organizational representative in order to communicate with the parents on a consistent basis in a non-combative and mutually agreed upon environment. Overall school goals will be discussed in detail in the next chapter.

B. Provide Off-Site Parental Meetings

If a large number of parents are living in a certain area, conduct meetings in a community center, church or other organization's facility near their homes, and offer child-care if there is more than one child in the family. If practical, offer transportation for those who need it because it is difficult for parents to obtain child-care and transportation in the evenings. Having access to these services makes the process easier for parents. I may sound somewhat biased in this area, but try opening the meeting with a motivational speaker who can inspire them by offering strategies regarding parenting to success, living their dreams, resolving conflicts, raising boys, etc. Because many times the ice is not broken at meetings, conflict occurs, so a connection exercise is an effective warm up. The key is to be creative in encouraging parents who have challenges connecting with the schools to create a win-win scenario instead of communicating only in times of conflict.

PROBLEM # 2—Perception That The American School System Is Not Supportive of Students of Color.

Many parents of color have developed notions, based upon their personal experiences, that the school system does not care for or support them and their children. When I was growing up, if one of my friends was having difficulty in school, parents immediately blamed the problem on the school system because it was hard for them to accept the fact that their child could really be the problem. Based upon my experiences, they had a right to be somewhat concerned because 80% of students expelled were students of color. These students spent a disproportionate amount of time in the principal's office, were usually reprimanded faster than their Caucasian peers, and were most likely to be "labeled." This still poses a major problem in the school systems because if parents do not regard the school as an asset to their children's lives, they will never know its true value. If they only see the school as a problematic entity, everyone loses, including their children. This must be fixed.

Possible Solutions

A. Develop parent surveys that allow parents to express their concerns.

Being proactive is key. The best way to prevent a fire is to have a fire plan. When my wife worked in a nuclear plant, one of her jobs was to design a plan for the facility in the event of a fire. She also had to develop fire prevention plans to minimize the impact of a possible fire by extinguishing it safely, early. Allowing parents to express their opinions and possible solutions in writing may be a way to connect with them in the community. A forum to analyze their answers in conjunction with this would enhance the concept even more. Simply inviting the parents into a meeting to request their input in improving the school may be one of the best ways to bond with the parents in an innovative way. My wife and I agree when raising children, to "teach in the time of non-confrontation." My advice in this scenario would be "to address issues in a time of non-confrontation" because during a confrontation, neither side listens very well.

B. Develop Parent Councils

The council development process was discussed earlier; another way to be proactive is to interact with parents who can assist you in connecting with uncommitted parents in the format of a council. The challenge, of course, will be getting everyone together, so meeting every other month may work best. The council will serve as a sounding board, and in some cases, a working board to unite parents and students. Some activities in which they could get involved are:

1. a parent-to-parent newsletter;
2. quarterly parents' rallies designed by the council;

3. e-zines, for technically minded parents;
4. school fund raisers for various projects;
5. trouble shooting for parenting challenges;
6. Much more, all developed by concerned parents!

A parent council is a great resource for connecting to parents in the school because the more they feel a sense of ownership of the school, the more involved they will become in its successful outcomes. This, too, will also help to change the negative perception many parents of color may have regarding the school.

C. Show Cultural Sensitivity

Consider the diverse cultures in your correspondence with the parents. Honor the various holidays and recognize some of the different traditions. For instance, Mexicans celebrate Cinco de Mayo, and African Americans celebrate Kwanzaa. Observing such holidays in the school in some fashion demonstrates that the school or organization is not one dimensional, and the children would enjoy the diversity as well.

Problem # 3—De-Motivated Staff

Even with all of the suggestions I have made and all of the information that your school or organization has gathered from other resources, if the team is not motivated to stay the course, you will always have problems. One of the most frequent complaints I hear from parents is the negative way they were treated. They felt disrespected and talked down to. If the staff is not motivated to follow through with ideas for change and is disrespectful, then the process will be extremely difficult. Commitment is a major key to short term and long term success.

Possible Solutions

A. Diversity Staff Retreats

A team getaway is an enticing strategy to motivate the staff towards goals. Much can be achieved in a focused, though temporary and relaxed environment. When working in the public sector, you will be faced with many "people challenges", but by proactively training the staff to handle certain challenges, you will learn that they can better negotiate situations that may occur in the school. Diversity training has been a term that has been overused but under-applied. Most people who are trained on diversity rarely follow through on what's been taught. That is why my company has always focused on the systems approach to training which is a foundation for the system that should be built in the school or organization. In order for success occur, a holistic viewpoint of success must be adopted by all in the organization; otherwise, year after year, the process will have to begin again, rather than continue to grow. A staff retreat is an effective way to get the ball rolling. If you have a strong parent council, you may want include the members in the retreat as well if that is acceptable according to school, district or organizational policy. This will really strengthen the bond between staff and parents.

B. Staff Recognition for Innovation

People by nature like incentives, so by providing them not as a cure all, but for ways to encourage innovation, many individuals will come up with creative ways to bridge the gap with parents. This technique is regularly used in corporate circles to increase sales and improve other areas of business. I am confident that it can also be used in the education arena to motivate staff members to employ creative thinking to reach and involve parents.

Summary

Hopefully some of these insights will work for you and your organization. Perhaps you have not realized, my heart is really the center of what I am sharing. I have committed my life to seeing our communities and people changed for the better, and I know that it is going to take creativity and ingenuity in order to make it happen. We have to move the old thought processes out of the way and open the door for new and positive perceptions. Parent connection is as important as student connection, so hopefully you will walk away from this chapter with enthusiasm for bridging the parent gap. It can be done. Simply start with committed people, who, through their enthusiasm, affect the hearts and minds of others. This is how all great movements began in this nation, one person at a time.

Key 6

—Bridging the Parent Gap Highlights—

- ✦ Establish goals with parents early in the year to give them a sense of accountability and meaningful inclusion in the educative process.

- ✦ Meet with parents in other locations besides your facility to better connect especially with single parents.

- ✦ Establish parent councils to get them involved.

- ✦ Take surveys to be proactive.

- ✦ Practice cultural sensitivity to break the ice on challenging relationships in the school and in the community.

Key 7

Developing Goals and Measurements

While speaking at a conference on closing the achievement gap in Virginia, I was asked by a school administrator my viewpoint on why we continue to have the same problems in the school systems year after year. He wondered why so many students of color continue to score low on standardized tests and what schools were doing wrong. I answered him referencing information shared about a program instituted in one of the toughest housing projects in Chicago. Youth, who were part of this unique program which had been in their community for less than a year, were questioned about its success. The interviewer asked, "So many programs in this community have failed time and time again, what is so different about this program?" The students, like a choir, replied in one voice, "Commitment." Individually, they replied, "They (faculty and staff) were committed to us and they never gave up on the program. "They had a goal to succeed and they did." "All of the other programs quit after a short period of time, but they stayed." I echo the statements of these outstanding youth in a different manner. The reason so many programs fail to reach our children is that the staff has more success concepts than heart to stay committed to the youth. They try one thing for a short while, but if it does not work immediately, they quit and go to something else. In other words, they have no solid goals for success, so anything goes. Since school challenges for students of color did not happen overnight, why do many people think we can fix it overnight? People in key positions in the academic community ask me "What is wrong with those kids? Why can't they just change?" I often pose a question of antiquated teaching methodologies: "Why can't they change?" If change were such an easy process, I would not need to write this book. There would not be a need for any self-help books, diet books, parenting books etc. But since change is a process, there is a need to be focused, committed, and connected. The bottom-line? Organizations need to have measurable goals that they are tenacious about achieving. There needs to be corporate buy-in to these goals, and great leadership in order to see long-term success. Since no two schools or organizations are the same, each one needs to come up with its own creative ideologies for success. There is no other way. You need goals, and you need to stick to them until you start to experience success. You may have to calibrate the goals from time to time, but you do need them in order to succeed.

Why Are Goals Important?

Imagine that there are 10 seconds left in the game. You are the star of the basketball team, and the point guard passes the ball for you to take the winning shot. You have perfect form: everything is going in slow motion; as the ball leaves your hand, you notice something interesting—there is no rim! Just an empty backboard. The clock winds down, the buzzer sounds, and your team loses the game. You argue with the referee who says there is nothing that you can do because the game is over. You reflect on the situation and ultimately ask your team and the fans, "How could I hit a target I never had? How could I score if there were no goal?" This anecdote illustrates the importance of having a target coupled with success measurement when you attempt to succeed. With no goal, you will simply sweat running up and down the court for no logical reason at all. These queries can be applied to schools and organizations which implement programs simply because they are told to do so. They do not have it in their heart to work toward change, but are only going through the motions. They have no goal, no direction, and no boundaries.

In order to stay motivated to positively impact students of color, you must set higher goals than the ones given to you. You must determine that you are not going to be average, but that you are going to be the best. It is this type of attitude that causes change to take place. "Attitude determines altitude." Though overused, this adage is very, very accurate.

Why Are Goals So Powerful?

When you establish goals for motivating students of color some questions are to be considered:

1. Why are we establishing these goals?
2. Are they realistic?
3. Do we have parental involvement?
4. What interpersonal challenges do our staff members have?
5. Who will lead various projects?
6. Where and how will we determine a benchmark?
7. Can we get 100% buy in?
8. What has worked or not worked in the past? How can we repeat the successes and learn from the failures?

Answers to all of these questions will help you to become more strategic as you write out a game plan and evaluate which approach is best. Concrete objectives will take the answers to these questions from concept to reality. When you commit to motivating students on a consistent basis, you need to focus on the task at hand because it is very easy to slip back into old mind-sets when a sufficient amount of structure is not in place. Goals, supported by concrete objectives, establish systems that can produce long- term success in motivating your students of color.

Why Do Measurements Matter?

I will not insult your intelligence, for you are the academic community; thus I am confident that you understand the process of using evaluative criteria to measure the achievement of objectives. I will say, however, that when you establish measurements for the objectives, your chances of success will grow exponentially. One of the primary reasons for the continued success of the HYPE Program is an ongoing process of measuring results weekly, monthly and quarterly. Learning to calibrate internal goals when you are not achieving the level of success that you are expecting will help you to stay on course to goal achievement. There are other important benefits as well.

1. Increased Group Enthusiasm

Goal attainment will bring a sense of pride and enthusiasm to any organization. Suppose your school or organization had 35% of your students of color pass the state exams one year? Implement goals to improve this number. Within two years the number could jump to 50%, within three years, to 60 % and by the next year, 80%. This is momentum—the kind of momentum that increases a sense of pride within team: parents, students and educators striving together to reach goals established by the team.

2. Increased Student Commitment

Many people remember *Lean on Me,* a fact-based film in which the new principal of a school was considered by many a tyrant. However, he had an objective; although his methods were tough, he forced the issue of change. Through his efforts, that school in New Jersey developed a committed staff and committed students. I am not in any way endorsing his model, but I am pointing out that the film does show that kids commit to people who commit to them. Often children of color don't commit because they do not see people as committed to them. Please remember that, to many, perception is reality; so even though you may think you are committed, if the students are not convinced, your efforts are somewhat in vain. If you set goals and have measurements for those goals, youth will start to take your initiatives seriously, then you will get their buy-in.

3. Historical Perspectives

By establishing solid goals for motivating students of color, you begin to establish success benchmarks. Your now have a point of success that you can use to measure ongoing programmatic success. As you are evaluating your initiatives, reflect on the processes you put in place and use them as a guideline for continuing to move forward. There is no success like your own, and by defining goals and measurements, you will without question start to see success. This is historically true.

Key Goals to Consider

When motivating students of color, I recommend a few specific goals for consideration based upon: years of classroom motivation programs; educator, parent, counselor, principal and administrator events; a multitude of keynote speeches; and the success of our HYPE workshops. By setting and committing to goals in these three areas, you will no doubt see success in motivating students of color.

GOAL #1—The Goal of Listening

This may seem like a simple goal to consider, but every organization needs to take it seriously. Often the answers to problems we face are screaming loudly at us everyday, but because we are not truly *listening*, we only *hear* them. With all of the activities that take place in a school day, all of the last minute "fires", all of the behavioral challenges, testing accountability etc., it is understandable that many educators feel stressed and anxious. However, in order to move beyond the stage of challenges to the stage of success, we must first seek to understand before being understood, according to Dr. Steven Covey author of *Seven Habits of Highly Effective People*. We can do this by listening to colleagues, parents, students, and our community. When crafting a plan to motivate students towards academic and personal excellence, view success from several vantage points. The vantage point of one of the stakeholders can be the key necessary to see the program succeed. When my firm initiated the HYPE Program, we, as a committed team, designed all of the workshop activities. We did not ask for much outside input for we were seeing some success and felt as though our program was all right as it was. Years later, we came up with the idea of youth inclusion in program development. Although this was initially an uncomfortable position for us to be in, we found later that is was one of the best ideas we had ever come up with, because by getting student input, our programs became more successful than our original events. By setting a goal to listen to what all of the participants are saying, you find that program implementation is easier and long-term success more likely.

GOAL # 2—The Goal of a Systematic Approach

As a former athlete, I have found that the players who had the greatest level of success had a systematic way of operation: their training regimens were systematic; the way they learned the plays were systematic; and the way they operated on the field or court was systematic. Although they would make adjustments when necessary, they had a routine and they adhered to it. They planned each step of the way, and maintained their plan. Other players who had no system would just "wing it." These players typically had short-term success if any success at all, and most of them had brief careers. Set the goal of having a systematic approach to motivating your students of color. Consider the meetings which must take place, the key personnel who will help to make it happen, a universal methodology that must be accepted by all on board, and what role students and others will play. The systematic approach will bring your organization success that the non-systematic approach will not.

GOAL 3—The Goal of Success

This, too, may seem like a simple goal, but it is actually a very profound one. Why set a goal if you do not plan to be successful? When I set the goal of doing what I do today, I had only one major goal—to succeed significantly. Refusing to become a small business casualty, I set the goal that we would succeed and positively impact lives worldwide. We are now doing this in our organization because failure is not a consideration. Nothing less than success will suffice. What does success look like for your school or organization? Put it in writing so that everyone can see it concretely, regularly. Is it improved test scores? better relationships? an increased number of students graduating? improved cultural sensitivity? Share it with everyone. Motivational expert Zig Ziglar states that, "There are two types of goals—Give up goals and— Go up goals. Give up goals you share with your closest friends. Go up goals you share with everyone." Since your desire is to go up, share it with everyone! Get everyone motivated about your plans. You can do it! We know you can!

Summary

This is the last key. A key is a powerful tool because it unlocks the lock. This implies that if you do not have a key, you cannot unlock the lock on the chest containing the answers to your problems. I have called them keys because I believe that if you have the keys you can unlock the lock and release the power of student motivation. You can begin to see success in areas you once deemed hopeless. You can begin to see the world as I do, where all people, regardless of race or creed, can become viable, productive citizens. This is why we "Believe the HYPE." It is our hope you are now on the HYPE Bandwagon, the one that is determined to transform our school systems in such a way, that there will no longer be a need for closing the achievement gap conferences, no child left behind legislation, school police, minority student grants or anything of the sort. We will live in a nation where success is the norm for all and failure is unacceptable. Hopefully you now "Believe the HYPE"—that all of our children can and will live their greatest dreams.

Key 7

—Developing Goals and Measurements Highlights—

+ In order to stay motivated to positively impact students of color, you must set higher goals than the ones given to you.

+ Many times the answers, to problems we face are screaming loudly at us everyday; however, because we are not *listening*, we only *hear* them.

+ What does success look like for your school or organization? Write it down, so that everyone can see it concretely, regularly.

Chapter 9

Closing the Achievement Gap— Latino and African American Student Perspectives

Years ago I shared the concept of youth councils with organizations all over the nation. Unfortunately, my enthusiasm for the concept was not received in the manner in which I thought appropriate. I would hear things such as "We know what is best for the youth," and "They do not know enough to provide good input." I would regularly say to organizations that it is critical for you to get feedback from your students. Listed below are four solid reasons for my insistence on this point:

1. When young people become a part of the solution, they will not be part of the problem. They can provide adults with advice that they would not have thought of on their own.
2. Adults have a tendency to forget their youthful days, or simply try to rationalize the shortcomings of their younger years.
3. Today's youth are much smarter and innovative than we give them credit for.
4. When young people take ownership and feel included, their outlook on life improves and their determination to succeed intensifies.

Because I believe that young people can help, this chapter is dedicated to obtaining advice from young people as it relates to closing the achievement gap. My company interviewed various youth who experienced our H.Y.P.E. Program; all of the students interviewed were Black or Latino. Included below are their responses to the questions posed. To ensure their privacy, I will not reveal their names; however, I will indicate whether the comment was from a Black or Latino perspective. Hopefully this information will shed some light on the thoughts of today's youth relevant to closing the achievement gap.

QUESTION #1
Why do you think that there is a nationwide problem with students of color excelling in the classroom?

Black Student—*"It is your surroundings. If everyone is on the corner, that is where you are going to be. Many of us are affected by our relationships."*

Latino Student—*"No connection to cultural heritage. The classroom doesn't make sense based upon my world."*

Black Student—*"There's an attitude in my community that education isn't important. It is generally accepted, so most people don't take school seriously. For those of us who try, we are labeled in some way. It's not easy."*

Latino Student—*"Caucasian teachers are scared of us. They see us as criminals and problems."*

QUESTION #2
What are the schools doing wrong?

Latino Student—*"When I arrived in America I was very proficient in Math. I found that there was a strong emphasis on ESL but little on math and other proficiencies. I was placed in a lower grade level math due to the language barrier. No one took the time to consider ways for me to stay in the level of math I obtained while in my native country. It seemed to me that the system was only concerned about their needs; they were not interested in mine at all. I was humiliated and it really affected my self-esteem. If people would consider differences in people and attempt to work with them, we would see an increase in student of color performance. I am now 19 years old and a junior in college. This proves I have the skills to succeed, so do many other Latinos."*

Black Student—*"Teachers act like they are not interested in being there. They are not highly motivated. Many times is seems as though they are there for the money only."*

Latino Student—*"Many people due to the cultural differences assume many things about us. One thing I find is that we are often encouraged to find jobs after high school. I have dreams for college and beyond, however I am looked at differently because I am Latino. Schools need to help teachers better understand ways to motivate all students, not just the students they consider their 'favorites'. This would help close the gap."*

Black Student—*"I think it is because of how people see us. People have perceptions of us that are not too positive."*

Black Student—*"Some teachers do not support you. They do not have the time to teach you. If you cause a problem, they are quick to get rid of you."*

QUESTION #3
Why do the Asians and Caucasians outscore students in test?

Latino Students—*"They are expected to do well and we are not. Because of this, they do well and we don't. You do what people expect of you!"*

Black Student—*"They have a history of success. Their minds have been programmed this way before the days of slavery in the USA. They have an advantage."*

QUESTION #4
What positive qualities do you see in educators who believe in you?

Latino Student—*"They help us. They support you. They help you take responsibility."*

Black Student—*"They work with us in our level. They are aware of who we are and are aware of our challenges. They know we are young and don't talk down to us."*

QUESTION #5
What can schools do to help students of color excel academically?

Black & Latino Students—*"Hire more teachers of color. We need to see more people who look like us teaching in the classroom. We need to see more people of color come in and talk to us. We believe that teachers of color will be more compassionate relating to what we need. Not that the teachers cannot teach us if they are Caucasian; however if that is all we have, how can they be familiar with the struggles we face on a day to day basis?"* (A compilation of answers)

Black Student—*"Teachers need to be trained. They need to better understand how we operate. They need to understand our world better."*

Latino Student—*"I like American history but I am tired of talking about George Washington, Teddy Roosevelt and other historical white Americans. My people have a history in this nation too, but I never hear of them. It would make a big difference if I saw the school systems take the time to consider our history and make it a requirement for all of the class to study, just like we have to study their history."*

Black Student—*"Stop labeling us. Look at us as equal."*

QUESTION #6
What role do parents play?

Black and Latino—*"They play an important role. Even though we are not excited when they show up to our schools, we know that it is important for them to be there."*

FINAL QUESTION
What is one piece of advice you can give to the school systems to close the achievement gap?

Latino and Black Students:

+ Provide support.
+ Be effective at leadership.
+ Help students if they are having a problem.
+ Start to connect with us at a younger age.
+ Work on communicating with us. Be effective.
+ Understanding where we are.
+ Encourage us always.
+ Stay focused on success.

Summary

My goal in this chapter has been to open your eyes to the truth, the truth that our youth of color have developed perceptions about the problems we are facing in today's education system— problems that we cannot continue to ignore. These problems are not going to be resolved by higher and tougher standards, remediation, special education, or other resources that are common to students of color and school systems. Instead, the problems are going to be resolved by caring people who see this as a mission, not merely a job. All kids need love and support from those who have the ability to impact their lives daily. They need a support structure in the home, school and community that will provide them with a sense of hope in making their dreams reality.

In my line of work, frequently I detect a lot of stress and frustration in those whom I serve as a speaker, trainer or consultant. Understanding their challenges, I always begin by assuring them that there is hope. Through implementing effective systems, there is hope. Through practicing regular introspection, there is hope. Through loving and caring for tomorrow's leaders, there is hope. Hope—when it arrives—gives life to the recipient, so never give up on the hope that your students of color can excel academically and personally. This chapter was designed to hopefully help many understand what the students are thinking but not saying openly. We need to listen more often. As a parent, I have more success listening than talking. So when I talk, I am more effective because I have listened. Hear the real words behind the hearts of your students. By more efficiently connecting with students, collaborating with parents, engaging the community and developing a passionate attitude about student success, you will undoubtedly succeed. Not only will you help to close the achievement gap, you will close the dream gap. More of our students will feel comfortable about believing in and pursuing their dreams, which in turn will make our world a better place. Success starts with the heart and grows with your love and compassion. Your students, children, friends, and this nation are depending on you. As Dr. Myles Munroe declared, "One person with courage is a majority." Become that majority! Never give up until you achieve the gold medal forged out of love, compassion, and student dreams fulfilled!

—Chapter 9 Highlights—

✦ Because I believe young people can make contributions to their effective development, this chapter has been dedicated to getting advice from them as it relates to closing the achievement gap.

✦ The problems educators and mentors face will not be resolved by higher and tougher standards, remediation, special education or other resources that are common to school systems which deal with students of color.

✦ Success starts with the heart and continues with your love and compassion. Your students, children, friends, and this nation are depending on you as mentors and educators.

✦ By better connecting with your students, collaborating with parents, engaging the community and developing a passionate attitude about student achievement, success is inevitable.

Closing Thoughts

Because I am passionate about my work, with a wife and family to support, I still left the comfort of a corporate job in order to make a difference. For a transformation to occur, it sometimes takes a radical, determined person to be a trailblazer. I consider myself a trailblazer. To many of you my thoughts may seem somewhat unorthodox and outlandish, but in my research I noticed that it was the radical people who had the greatest impact on history. Consider the Wright brothers' belief that man should fly. They lived their passionate dream even though many people considered them insane. Two boys from Dayton, Ohio are the foundation for 80% of the economic and worldwide power we see today, for where would we be without airplanes and space exploration? Madame C.J. Walker revolutionized business for African-Americans. She was a successful entrepreneur and millionaire despite being one generation removed from slavery. Where would we be if it weren't for the Madame and her inspiration to African American business owners? Alexander Graham Bell almost went bankrupt attempting to prove that telecommunications could become a reality. He and his partner Watson committed their passion to one invention that revolutionized the world. Marva Collins' charter school proved that all young African Americans can learn if properly motivated. More schools could adopt her philosophy and succeed. There are many more examples, but I think you see my point. Nothing takes place unless people are determined enough to see change and transformation. We cannot afford to continue down the same racially divided roads that traditionally have been traveled. We are all equal and should all be given a fair chance to live our dreams: the dreams that we can have a family, secure a passionate career, have a positive impact on society, and provide examples to the next generation. Unless someone hammers this point home, I believe that we will be doomed to go down paths of failure indefinitely.

Our children of color can, will, and must succeed because their ancestors were vital in the building of this nation and other nations. They have a right to go for the gold without all the limitations and stereotypes that are pinned to them. It is this belief in their abilities that will cause them to succeed. By doing this, we will begin to see a brighter future for us all. That young man that is challenging you today could one day grow up to become a tenacious lawyer. That young lady who seems to not focus in class could one day grow up to become a great artist expressing her creative and imaginative mind. In changing our paradigms to this perception of students, we begin to see them in a successful light.

Become a trailblazer with me. Do not go the road most traveled; go the one less traveled, and in doing this you confirm that you do "Believe the HYPE"—the HYPE that your students can and will succeed. Be willing to take that responsibility personally. Let's do it together. Let's empower the next generation of leaders by loving them to success. Ralph Waldo Emerson urged, "Don't go where the path may lead, instead go where there is no path, and leave a trail." You are a trailblazer!

Darrell "Coach D" Andrews
Consultant ✦ Speaker ✦ Trainer

Middle & High School Programs

- ✦ Career Development
- ✦ Leadership, Teambuilding & Diversity Workshops
- ✦ School Assemblies
- ✦ Senior Year Transition
- ✦ Parent Programs

Educator Programs

- ✦ Working with At-Risk Youth
- ✦ Closing the Achievement Gap
- ✦ Connecting Dreams to Education
- ✦ Leadership, Teambuilding & Diversity Workshops

CALL US AT: 1-866-4-Coach-D
or (302) 328-3690

VISIT US ONLINE AT: www.CoachDSpeaks.com

OR EMAIL US AT: info@CoachDSpeaks.com

WRITE TO US AT: Darrell Andrews Enterprises, Inc.
1148 Pulaski Highway
Suite 197
Bear, DE 19701

We want to hear from you. Share your story
about how this book or a training/speaking program
conducted by Coach D has changed your life or the life
of your students. You may email us or write to us
at the address above. We would love to hear from you!

Order Form

MAIL THIS FORM AND PAYMENT TO:

Darrell Andrews Enterprises, Inc.
1148 Pulaski Hwy., Suite 197
Bear, DE 19701
or fax this form to: (302) 832-6127

SHIP TO:

_____
NAME

_____
ADDRESS

_____
CITY   STATE   ZIP

_____
TELEPHONE   EMAIL

How To Find Your Passion And Make A Living At It (ISBN 0-9660103-3-7)	$12.95	
The Purpose Living Teen (ISBN 0-9660103-8-8)	$12.95	
Believing The HYPE: 7 Keys to Motivating Students of Color (ISBN 0-9660103-5-3)	$12.95	
HYPE School of Dreams (ISBN 0-9660103-7-x)	$149.95	
Chicken Soup for the African American Soul (ISBN: 0-7573-0142-8)	$14.95	
	SUBTOTAL	
Add 30% of product total for shipping charges SHIPPING		
	TOTAL	

PAYMENT INFORMATION:

☐ Check or Money Order (Payable to Darrell Andrews Enterprises, Inc.)

☐ Bill my credit card # _____

☐ Visa   ☐ MC   ☐ AmEx   Exp. Date_____

Signature_____

☐ Purchase Order # _____

Please allow 4 to 6 weeks for US delivery. Prices are subject to change without notice.